SINGAPORE HAWKER CLASSICS UNVEILED

Decoding 25 Favourite Dishes

Supported by

Project manager: Glenn Wray
Editor: Lydia Leong
Photographer: Hongde Photography

Copyright © 2015 Temasek Polytechnic

Reprinted 2016, 2017, 2019, 2021, 2022

Published by Marshall Cavendish Cuisine
An imprint of Marshall Cavendish International

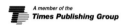

Other Marshall Cavendish Offices:
Marshall Cavendish Corporation, 800 Westchester Ave, Suite N-641, Rye Brook, NY 10573, USA
• Marshall Cavendish International (Thailand) Co Ltd, 253 Asoke, 16th Floor, Sukhumvit 21 Road, Klongtoey Nua, Wattana, Bangkok 10110, Thailand • Marshall Cavendish (Malaysia) Sdn Bhd, Times Subang, Lot 46, Subang Hi-Tech Industrial Park, Batu Tiga, 40000 Shah Alam, Selangor Darul Ehsan, Malaysia

Marshall Cavendish is a registered trademark of Times Publishing Limited

National Library Board, Singapore Cataloguing-in-Publication Data

Singapore hawker classics unveiled : decoding 25 favourite dishes / Temasek Polytechnic. –
Singapore : Marshall Cavendish Cuisine, [2015]
pages cm
ISBN : 978-981-4677-65-3
1. Cooking, Singaporean. 2. Cookbooks. I. Temasek Polytechnic, author.
TX724.5.S55
641.595957 -- dc23   OCN908329136

Printed in Singapore

CONTENTS

FOREWORD

It is well known that we Singaporeans love our food! How could it be otherwise when we can enjoy such delectable hawker fare as laksa, *roti prata* and chicken rice readily and regularly? At Temasek Polytechnic, we are as obsessed with food as anyone, and this unique book, *Singapore Hawker Classics Unveiled: Decoding 25 Favourite Dishes* is testament to that.

It is fitting that we publish the book this year in 2015, the year Singapore celebrates her 50th birthday as an independent nation. It is double celebration for Temasek Polytechnic as we commemorate our own 25th anniversary in conjunction with Singapore's Golden Jubilee. We have deliberately selected 25 dishes to feature in this book — one for every year of our history.

Singapore's culinary heritage should be treasured and preserved. A good way to do this is by nurturing future generations of culinary masters. At Temasek Polytechnic, we contribute to the pool of culinary talent through our Diploma in Baking and Culinary Science and Diploma in Culinary and Catering Management programmes.

The 25 specially selected recipes featured in this book will allow you to recreate your favourite classic hawker treats at home and inspire you to look at these familiar dishes in a new light — each dish includes its traditional presentation together with an additional interpretation with a modern twist. Every dish is covered in meticulous detail, including information on its heritage, its aroma, taste and texture, its nutritional value, as well as clear step-by-step instructions and photographs.

So it gives us great pleasure to present you with this book. We hope you enjoy trying out the recipes and uncovering new nuggets and other secrets surrounding Singapore's classic hawker delights.

Boo Kheng Hua
Principal & CEO
Temasek Polytechnic

ACKNOWLEDGEMENTS

Temasek Polytechnic would like to express its gratitude to all those who have helped make this book possible, notably through grants provided by the SG50-Education & Youth Committee (EYC) Collaboration Fund, as well as the Heritage Participation Grant from the National Heritage Board.

We would also like to thank Lau Choy Seng Pte Ltd and Sia Huat Pte Ltd for generously providing us with the beautiful flatware used in this book.

Yet the biggest thanks are reserved for the hard-working team of staff, students and graduates from the Diploma in Baking and Culinary Science at Temasek Polytechnic who meticulously prepared the content — it is a considerable achievement to be proud of. Thank you.

INTRODUCTION

With two significant milestones taking place in 2015 — Singapore's 50th birthday (SG50) and Temasek Polytechnic's 25th anniversary (TP25) — how best can we commemorate these events, but in the true-blue Singaporean way, by focusing on our favourite subject matter, FOOD. A true reflection of our rich heritage and colourful multicultural society, food is the one aspect that will always draw people from different walks of life and different ethnicities together.

This compilation consists of 25 favourite hawker dishes that every Singaporean would be familiar with. These dishes would also be on any visitor's list of must-try foods while in Singapore. From main dishes to desserts, the list showcases the best that each ethnic and cultural group in Singapore has to offer.

This book was first conceptualised in 2010 when Professor Tommy Koh, then the Chairman of the National Heritage Board, called for Singapore hawker food to be taught in culinary schools to address the pressing need to preserve the integrity of our hawker dishes. Considering the possible lack of understanding and therefore the lack of interest among our youths concerning local food culture, the team from the Diploma in Baking and Culinary Science at Temasek Polytechnic took on the challenge to decipher Singapore's favoured 25 hawker dishes and share them in this book, with the aim of getting our youths immersed in the local food culture. Tapping on the course's technical capabilities in culinary and science, the development of this book saw students, graduates and staff (also from the Library and Information Resources Department) putting in many hours of hard work to explore and rediscover our favourite hawker dishes.

The end result is this book that you now hold in your hands. Each recipe starts with a record of the origins of the dish and the variations and similar dishes that are available within Singapore and around the region. The sensory attributes of the dish are also provided to give the reader a sense of its aroma, flavour profile and mouthfeel, together with the tried and tested recipe. Important steps of the recipe are highlighted with photographs to better illustrate the technique. Though some recipes are not traditionally prepared, these have been adapted for ease of preparation to obtain optimum results and ensure reproducibility of the recipe.

The energy and nutrient contributions of each dish are also tabulated for the discerning and health-conscious reader. Additional gems include the scientific explanation relating to an ingredient or cooking technique to provide a deeper understanding. Finally, each dish is given an alternative presentation, yet still preserving its essence as a catalyst for the modern cooking enthusiast or young culinary explorer.

In working on this book, the team at Temasek Polytechnic rediscovered our own passion for Singapore's culinary heritage. We hope this book will also help our youths and anyone reading this book to ignite their passion for Singapore's hawker food and keep this rich food culture alive for many years to come.

Rice and Noodles

Beef Kway Teow

This beef noodle soup, is popularly known as beef *kway teow* or *gu bak kway teow*. It is a traditional Southern Chinese street dish of beef slices and/or innards and brisket with rice noodles in a beef broth.

Beef *kway teow* usually refers to the Teochew version which traditionally consists of flat rice noodles (*kway teow*), beef slices (and the options of tripe, brisket, and tendons) scalded in beef stock or water, bean sprouts, and a dark and robust soup. The soup is made from boiling beef bones and herbs and spices, such as cloves, black peppercorns, palm sugar and galangal, and enhanced with condiments such as soya sauce.

Beef *kway teow* is typically garnished with coriander and served with preserved mustard cabbage (*kiam chye*) and a chilli sauce topped with shredded or pounded galangal.

Origins
Beef noodle soup was sold by Chinese vendors in Singapore as early as the 1920s and is still predominantly sold by Chinese vendors today. Although thought to be a traditional Teochew dish that originated from China, there are other versions of this dish from the Hakka and Hainanese communities, as well as hybrids of the different versions.

Variations and similar dishes
In Singapore, the traditional Hainanese version of beef noodles uses thick rice vermicelli (*chor bee hoon*) and comes smothered in dark viscous gravy made from beef stock, dark soya sauce, aniseed, cinnamon and cloves, and is topped with either beef slices, beef tendons, tripe, beef balls, or a combination of these. The dish is then garnished with coriander and/or diced preserved mustard cabbage (*kiam chye*), and, sometimes, a sprinkling of crushed peanuts. Hainanese beef noodles is served with a chilli sauce that contains fermented shrimp sauce (*cincalok*) and lime juice.

The Hakka community in Singapore also has a dish of beef noodle soup. However, this dish is very different from the Teochew and Hainanese versions as the noodles — rice vermicelli (*bee hoon*), flat rice noodles (*kway teow*) or egg noodles — are served with a light, clear soup with beef balls or sliced beef. The chilli sauce that is served with the noodles is made with bird's eye chilli (*cili padi*), garlic and rice wine.

SCIENCE CONNECTION

Simmering the beef parts for an extended period of time allows the collagen present in the meat tissues to be converted to gelatin. During braising or stewing, meat and tendon start to lose their toughness when the temperature rises above 65°C. At such temperatures, the chemical bonds begin to break and form gelatin. The breakdown of collagen to gelatin makes the meat more tender.

Right: Alternative presentation of beef *kway teow* — beef velouté with braised tendons, beef tripe and dried Chinese mushrooms

Beef Kway Teow

Serves 4

AROMA
Dominantly beefy with a delicate blend of Chinese five-spice powder, garlic and ginger

FLAVOUR PROFILE
Savoury beef flavour with an umami-rich note and a hint of fresh coriander

MOUTHFEEL
Springy, smooth rice noodles in a rich broth contrasted with the tender and chewy beef offals and meat

---

Beef bones **400 g**

1. Boil a pot of water and blanch beef bones to remove impurities.
2. Drain and rinse with cold water. Set aside.

Water **2.5 L**
Beef flank, cut into bite-size pieces **250 g**
Beef tendons **100 g**
Beef tripe **100 g**
Beef balls, cooked **8**
Ginger **10 g**
Garlic, skin on **12 g / 3 cloves**
Salt **10 g / 2 tsp**
Chinese five-spice powder **4 g / 1 tsp**
Black pepper powder **2.5 g / ¹/₂ tsp**

3. Combine ingredients, except for beef balls, with blanched beef bones in a large pot.
4. Bring to a boil, then lower heat and simmer for about 3 hours.
5. Add beef balls before turning off heat.
6. Skim off any residue if necessary.

Dark soya sauce **12 g / 2 tsp**

7. Season soup and keep hot.

Flat rice noodles (*kway teow*) **400 g**
Bean sprouts **80 g**

8. Boil a pot of water and blanch ingredients separately for 15 to 20 seconds.
9. Drain and portion into serving bowls.

Coriander leaves **15 g / 2 sprigs**
Calamansi limes, halved **4**

10. Ladle beef soup over noodles with equal amounts of beef flank, tendons, tripe and beef balls.
11. Garnish with coriander leaves and calamansi limes.
12. Serve hot.

NUTRITION PROFILE	PER SERVING
Energy (kcal)	352
Total fat (g)	8
Saturated fat (g)	3
Cholesterol (mg)	96
Carbohydrate (g)	49
Protein (g)	35
Dietary fibre (g)	<1
Sodium (mg)	1345

 CHEF'S ADVICE

For a richer and stronger flavoured broth, roast the beef bones in a 200°C oven for about 45 minutes or until the bones are brown before simmering.

Char Kway Teow

Char kway teow is the Hokkien term for fried flat rice noodles. It is a hawker dish consisting of noodles stir-fried over high heat with various ingredients and seasoned with dark soya sauce.

Char kway teow is considered to be a simple dish in terms of composition, but the difficulty lies is in the cooking. This is because the dish requires good control over the speed of cooking and the heat of the wok.

Traditionally, this dish was made to satisfy the stomachs of hard-working labourers such as fishermen, farmers and cockle-gatherers. The nutritional value of this dish meets the needs of these manual labourers, as it is high in carbohydrates, fat and salt to supply a substantial amount of energy to take on energy-dissipating jobs. It is often assumed that these labourers were the ones who created this dish and, due to their poor backgrounds, sold this dish part-time to supplement their income.

Based on this assumption, it is apparent why cockles were used in *char kway teow*. Cockles also add a unique flavour to the dish.

Origins

The exact origins of *char kway teow* are unknown, and a similar version is also served in Penang in Malaysia. However, *char kway teow* was known to have been a low cost dish eaten by labourers for additional energy through the day, and is thus likely to have originated as simple hawker fare for the poor in early Singapore. The original version of *char kway teow* is believed to have included only the fried noodles, cockles and dark soya sauce, so as to keep the cost low.

Variations

The modern version of *char kway teow* includes ingredients such as flat rice noodles (*kway teow*), sweet dark soya sauce, Chinese chives, fishcake, cockles, eggs, bean sprouts and Chinese sausages fried with pork lard for flavour.

The Penang version uses only rice noodles and light soya sauce, and is therefore not as dark or sweet. The Penang version also includes prawns and chives to add a seafood flavour to the dish, and is generally considered more savoury than the Singapore version.

SCIENCE CONNECTION

Traditionally, *char kway teow* is stirred in a seasoned cast iron wok over a high open flame to impart characteristic flavours to the dish. The flavour, which includes the taste and aroma, may be brought about by chemical compounds developed from caramelisation and Maillard reaction, as well as the partial combustion of oil when the food is seared at high temperatures. Achieving this flavour note is not simple and even chefs themselves require some experience and skill to create this effect.

Right: Alternative presentation of *char kway teow* — seafood *kway teow aglio olio*

Char Kway Teow

Serves 4

AROMA
Slight smoky aroma from the wok-fried noodles and garlic

FLAVOUR PROFILE
Savoury and sweet notes of the sweet sauce and Chinese sausages with occasional seafood flavour of cockles, and a slight eggy note

MOUTHFEEL
A combination of springy, smooth rice noodles and firm Hokkien noodles; with crunchy bean sprouts and chewy bits of Chinese sausage and fishcake

---

Water **150 mL**
Sweet dark soya sauce **65 g / 3½ Tbsp**
Dark soya sauce **50 g / 3 Tbsp**
Light soya sauce **10 g / 2 tsp**

1. Combine ingredients and mix well. Set seasoning mixture aside.

Corn oil **10 g / 1 Tbsp**
Pork lard, diced **30 g**
Garlic, peeled and minced **30 g / 10 cloves**

2. Heat oil in a wok over medium heat and fry pork lard.
3. Add garlic and stir-fry until golden brown.

Chinese sausages, thinly sliced **60 g**
Fried fishcake, thinly sliced **60 g**

4. Add Chinese sausages and fishcake. Stir-fry for 1 minute.

Flat rice noodles (*kway teow*) **400 g**
Yellow Hokkien noodles **100 g**

5. Add rice noodles and yellow Hokkien noodles. Toss for 1 minute until thoroughly mixed.
6. Add seasoning mixture and toss to mix.

Chye sim, cut into 5-cm lengths **100 g**
Bean sprouts **50 g**

7. Add vegetables and stir-fry for 1 minute.

Eggs, beaten **220 g / 4**
Cockles, shelled **60 g**

8. Push noodles to one side of the wok. Add eggs and stir to scramble.
9. Add cockles and toss for 20 seconds.
10. Portion out onto serving plates.
11. Serve hot.

NUTRITION PROFILE	PER SERVING
Energy (kcal)	562
Total fat (g)	19
Saturated fat (g)	6
Cholesterol (mg)	193
Carbohydrate (g)	72
Protein (g)	16.3
Dietary fibre (g)	<1
Sodium (mg)	1020

 CHEF'S ADVICE

Chinese sausages can be eaten with the waxy skin, but if you prefer to peel the skin away, soak the sausages in hot water for about 5 minutes. The waxy skin can then be peeled off easily.

Fried Hokkien Mee

Fried Hokkien *mee* is a dish of thick yellow wheat noodles cooked with rice vermicelli (*bee hoon*) or laksa noodles. (*Mee* is the Hokkien term for noodles.)

The name of the dish is a bit of a misnomer, as the noodles are not actually fried, but are instead simmered in stock to absorb its flavours. The dish is today ubiquitous in Singapore and is commonly accompanied with sambal *belacan* (chilli with dried shrimp paste) and calamansi lime.

Origins

The exact origins of fried Hokkien *mee* are unclear, but it has been said that the dish originated in the 1880s and was sold by Hokkien immigrants. The dish was also regarded a luxury in those days, and as such, the Chinese were not willing to pay to eat it. It was however a favoured dish among the Peranakans, Eurasians and Europeans.

Today, fried Hokkien *mee* is a relatively inexpensive hawker dish available throughout Singapore.

Another version as recorded in an oral history interview states that Rochor *mee* originated in the 1960s from a large market which occupied the area where the shopping mall, Bugis Junction, now stands. The market specialised in selling pork and there was often unsold pork at the end of the day, which the hawkers would cut into small strips and cook together with a sauce made from prawn shells. Lard from the market was also used to fry the noodles. Rochor *mee* therefore began as a dish to utilise inexpensive and unsold cuts of pork.

In the past, fried Hokkien *mee* was served in *opeh* 'leaves'. These are actually not leaves, but pieces of bark from the betel nut tree. *Opeh* was used to wrap the cooked dish for takeaway, and it was thought that the *opeh* helped preserve and impart flavour to the dish.

Variations

The modern version of the dish is made using a mixture of Hokkien noodles and thick rice vermicelli (*chor bee hoon*) or laksa noodles, cooked and simmered together in the stock. Other ingredients used include prawns, squid, chives, bean sprouts, eggs, deep-fried pieces of pork lard and pork belly. Some hawkers also include other ingredients, ranging from the relatively common fishcake and leafy green vegetables or, in more expensive versions of the dish, abalone or oysters.

Today, fried Hokkien *mee* is also often served with sambal *belacan* (chilli with dried shrimp paste) and calamansi lime, which was introduced by the Peranakans.

The original version of fried Hokkien *mee* is sometimes called the dry version as it had less gravy and stock. This version was cooked over a charcoal fire, but charcoal cooking has become rare in contemporary times due to the convenience of gas cookers. Fried Hokkien *mee* cooked over a charcoal stove was favoured for the smoky flavour which the charcoal imparted.

SCIENCE CONNECTION

Hokkien noodles, otherwise known as yellow alkaline noodles, is widely used in Asian cooking. Made from wheat flour, water, salt and sodium or potassium carbonate, the noodles gets its characteristic look and feel from the carbonate compound. Sodium or potassium carbonate increases the pH (alkalinity) of the noodle, causing the flour proteins to toughen, and a unique alkaline taste to be developed. The yellow colour comes about as the alkali causes a chemical reaction that converts the colourless flavonoids (pigments) to a yellowish hue. If the wheat flour has a high carotenoid content, the reaction will lead to brightly coloured yellow noodles.

Right: Alternative presentation of fried Hokkien *mee* — crispy Hokkien noodles

Fried Hokkien Mee

Serves 4

For chilli paste

Dried shrimp paste (*belacan*), dry-roasted **5 g**
Shallots, peeled **50 g**
Dried red chilli, soaked in warm water **1**
Fresh red chillies **25 g**
Garlic, peeled **3 g / 1 clove**
Candlenut **2 g / 1**

1. Combine ingredients in a blender and blend into a fine paste.

Corn oil **20 g / 2 Tbsp**

2. Heat oil in a wok over medium heat and fry chilli paste until it turns deep red and is fragrant.

Tamarind pulp **10 g**
Water **5 g / 1 tsp**

3. Combine ingredients and mix well. Strain to obtain 5 g tamarind juice.
4. Combine with fried chilli paste and set aside for serving with noodles.

For prawn stock

Pork bones **600 g**

5. Boil a pot of water and blanch pork bones to remove impurities.
6. Drain and rinse with cold water. Set aside.

Prawn shells and heads **200 g**
Water **2 L**
Pork belly, cut into 1-cm thick pieces **160 g**

7. In another wok, fry prawn shells and heads over high heat until golden orange and fragrant.
8. Add water, blanched pork bones and pork belly. Cover and simmer over low heat.
9. Remove pork belly after 20 minutes and continue to simmer remaining ingredients for another hour.
10. Skim off any residue if necessary.
11. Cut cooked pork belly into thin strips. Set aside.

For noodles

Prawns **16**
Squid **60 g**

12. Shell and devein prawns, leaving tails intact.
13. Clean squid. Pull off head with tentacles, intestines and quill. Peel off purple skin and fins. Reserve tentacles and fins for other use. Slice squid tube into rings.
14. Blanch prawns and squid for 15 to 20 seconds in prawn shell stock. Drain and cool.

Pork lard, diced **20 g**
Garlic, peeled and minced
   10 g / 3 cloves
Eggs, beaten **220 g / 4**
Yellow Hokkien noodles **300 g**
Thick rice vermicelli
   (*chor bee hoon*) **100 g**
Fish sauce **15 g / 1 Tbsp**

Bean sprouts **40 g**
Chinese chives, cut into
   2-cm lengths **15 g / 2 sprigs**

For garnishing
Calamansi limes, halved **2**

15. Heat a wok over medium heat and fry the pork lard until crispy.
16. Add garlic and fry until golden brown.
17. Turn heat to high, add eggs and scramble thoroughly.
18. Add noodles and fish sauce. Mix well.
19. Add prawn stock, prawns, pork belly and squid rings.
20. Cover and braise noodles until most of the stock has been absorbed.
21. Stir in bean sprouts and Chinese chives. Cook for 3 minutes.
22. Portion evenly onto serving plates. Serve hot with calamansi limes and chilli paste.

NUTRITION PROFILE	PER SERVING
Energy (kcal)	590
Total fat (g)	31
Saturated fat (g)	11
Cholesterol (mg)	427
Carbohydrate (g)	37
Protein (g)	40
Dietary fibre (g)	<1
Sodium (mg)	944

 CHEF'S ADVICE
Blanch yellow Hokkien noodles in boiling water for 10 seconds to remove the alkaline taste.

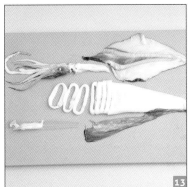

Hainanese Chicken Rice

In the Hainan Island of China, mother hens were used in this dish as the meat of these hens was succulent and rich in flavour. It was said that the best chicken for this dish was a local breed of chicken known as *wen chang* chicken.

The chicken has to be of a certain age — not too young so that the flesh is not bland, yet not old to be tough from age and egg-laying. The rice is cooked with the fat of the chicken, garlic, ginger and pandan leaves. Served steaming hot, the rice is unique with a nice tinge of yellow, and fragrant and full of flavour.

The chicken rice served today is garnished with a few slices of cucumber, sprigs of coriander, and accompanied with a specially prepared fresh chilli sauce, finely grated ginger and juice, and thick dark soya sauce. Over the years, the dish has evolved with different variations and is no longer just prepared and sold by the Hainanese.

Variations The variations to Hainanese chicken rice lies mostly in how the chicken is prepared. Soya sauce chicken rice is said to be the Cantonese version of Hainanese chicken rice. The chicken is cooked in a rich dark sauce prepared with spices which includes cinnamon and clove, and is sweetened with rock sugar.

Roasted chicken rice is prepared by seasoning the whole chicken with black pepper and salt, then hanging it to dry before it is deep-fried until the skin is golden brown and crispy.

Chicken rice is so well-received that every hawker centre or food court in Singapore is likely to feature the dish. These days, chicken rice is served with thinly sliced cucumber and a specially prepared chilli sauce, thick dark soya sauce and ginger sauce. A bowl of soup made using the chicken stock usually accompanies the dish.

Condiments can include achar (a pineapple, cucumber and carrot pickle, with crushed peanuts and toasted white sesame seeds), braised bean curd, braised hard-boiled chicken egg or a plate of bean sprouts.

Hainanese chicken rice is also popular in Hong Kong, Thailand, Malaysia and Indonesia. In Hong Kong and Thailand, plain rice is served in place of the ginger-flavoured rice.

SCIENCE CONNECTION

Ginger (*Zingiber officinale*) is not a root but a rhizome or a stem of a plant that grows underground. The pungency of ginger is due to the presence of a group of essential oils called gingerols. Frying the ginger helps to boost the pungency and taste by causing gingerols to dehydrate and results in a stronger taste due to another group of compounds known as shogaol.

Right: Alternative presentation of Hainanese chicken rice
— chicken rice risotto with garlic-ginger purée

Hainanese Chicken Rice

Serves 4

AROMA
Fragrant garlic and sesame aroma with a hint of pandan

FLAVOUR PROFILE
Rich savoury chicken flavour with an umami note of soya sauce, accompanied with the garlic and ginger flavours of the rice

MOUTHFEEL
Tender, succulent chicken with moist yet firm rice that is slightly oily

For chicken

Whole chicken **1.2 kg**

1. Wash and clean cavity. Remove fat and set aside for later use.

Whole garlic, crushed **30 g / 10 cloves**
Ginger, sliced **10 g**
Spring onion **25 g / 1 sprig**

2. Stuff ingredients into cavity of chicken.

Water **4 L**
Pandan leaves, cleaned and knotted **4**
Coriander leaves, cut into 3-cm lengths **15 g / 2 sprigs**

3. Combine ingredients in a big pot and bring water to a boil. Submerge chicken, breast-side down, in the boiling water.
4. Turn off heat, cover pot and poach chicken for 1 hour. After cooking, pierce the thickest part of chicken thigh with a small knife. The juices should run clear. If not, cook for another 15 minutes over low heat.
5. Remove chicken from pot and reserve cooking liquid for preparation of rice, soup, chilli and ginger sauces. Submerge chicken in iced water for 30 minutes.
6. Discard ingredients in cavity. Chop chicken into serving portions. Place on a serving plate.
7. Garnish with coriander leaves.

For topping sauce

Light soya sauce **30 g / 2 Tbsp**
Dark soya sauce **6 g / 1 tsp**
Sesame oil **5 g / 2 tsp**

8. Combine ingredients and mix well.
9. Ladle over chicken to serve.

For rice

Corn oil **10 g / 1 Tbsp**
Chicken fat **35 g**

10. Heat oil in a pot over medium heat and render chicken fat.

Whole garlic, peeled and crushed **40 g**
Whole shallots, peeled **40 g**
Ginger, sliced **25 g**

11. Add to pot and stir-fry until fragrant.

Jasmine rice, uncooked **300 g**
Chicken cooking liquid **380 mL**
Pandan leaves, cleaned and knotted **4**
Salt **3 g / ¹/₂ tsp**

12. Rinse rice under running water and drain.
13. Add to pot and stir-fry until translucent.
14. Transfer to a rice cooker and add remaining ingredients. Cook rice.
15. Serve hot.

Thick dark soya sauce (for chicken rice) **60 g / 4 Tbsp**

16. Serve with chicken rice.

For chilli sauce

Fresh red chillies **20 g**
Ginger **10 g**
Garlic, peeled **3 g**

17. Combine ingredients in a blender and blend into a smooth paste.

Sesame oil **15 g / 1¹/₂ Tbsp**
Salt **3 g / ¹/₂ tsp**
Sugar **5 g / 1 tsp**
Lime juice **4 g / 1 tsp**
Hua diao jiu **2 g / ¹/₂ tsp**
Chicken cooking liquid **20 g /
    1¹/₂ Tbsp**

18. Combine ingredients in a mixing bowl and mix well.
19. Add chilli-ginger-garlic paste and stir to incorporate.
20. Serve at room temperature.

For ginger sauce

Ginger, sliced **50 g**
Salt **3 g / ¹/₂ tsp**
Garlic oil **3 g / 1 tsp**
Chicken cooking liquid **40 g /
    3 Tbsp**

21. Blend ginger into a fine paste.
22. Add salt and garlic oil and mix well.
23. Gradually add chicken cooking liquid and mix well.
24. Serve at room temperature.

For soup

Chicken cooking liquid **600 mL**
Salt **to taste**

25. Bring to a boil in a pot.
26. Serve with chicken rice.

NUTRITION PROFILE	PER SERVING
Energy (kcal)	643
Total fat (g)	23
Saturated fat (g)	6
Cholesterol (mg)	196
Carbohydrate (g)	52
Protein (g)	58
Dietary fibre (g)	1
Sodium (mg)	670

 CHEF'S ADVICE

Once the rice is cooked, set it aside for 10 minutes before fluffing it up. Letting the cooked rice rest will help keep the grains intact.

Indian Mee Goreng

Mee goreng literally translates as "fried noodles" in Malay. It is a classic Indian Muslim dish of stir-fried yellow Hokkien noodles, and is usually coloured a bright orange-red.

Although the name is Malay, *mee goreng* is a hybrid dish with influences from the Chinese and the Southern Indian communities. The noodles and ingredients are stir-fried in a wok with condiments, spices and fresh chillies or sambal chilli, with the chilli sauce and tomato ketchup giving the dish its distinctive bright orange-red hue. *Mee goreng* usually has a slightly charred flavour and look, and is typically served with slices of cucumber and a dollop of tomato sauce.

Origins

It has been suggested that *mee goreng* was sold in Singapore as early as before World War II by Indian migrants from Tamil Nadu who set up tea stalls known as *sarabat* stalls. Other sources suggest that *mee goreng* started as a street food item in the 1950s and that the earliest *mee goreng* stall started in Penang, Malaysia.

Despite its association with the Indian community, *mee goreng* did not originate from India. It was created by the locals using ingredients, spices and condiments from various cultures. This includes Hokkien noodles and firm bean curd (*tau kua*) from the Chinese, chillies, curry powder and minced meat, usually mutton, from the Malays and Indians, and boiled potatoes, tomato ketchup and chilli sauce from the West.

Variations and similar dishes

There are Chinese and Malay versions of *mee goreng*. Malay *mee goreng* is very similar to Indian *mee goreng* except for the absence of tomato sauce.

Mee kuah is considered the Chinese version of *mee goreng*. The same Hokkien noodles are used, served in a thick mutton soup (or *kuah*, the word for "gravy" in Hokkien) of marrow bones, chillies and tomatoes.

Variations of *mee goreng* include *nasi goreng* (fried rice), *bee hoon goreng* (fried rice vermicelli) and *kway teow goreng* (fried flat rice noodles), where the Hokkien noodles are substituted with different types of noodles or rice.

SCIENCE CONNECTION

The key compound responsible for the signature mutton flavour is 4-methyloctanoic acid, a branched-chain fatty acid produced in the liver of lambs. Those who do not enjoy this flavour may consider adding cooking wine to reduce it. The ethanol in cooking wine will react with 4-methyloctanoic acid at high temperature, forming an ester that is odourless.

Right: Alternative presentation of *mee goreng* — fettuccine *goreng* with pickled cucumber and mini lamb kebab

Indian Mee Goreng

Serves 4

AROMA
A light ketchup and chilli aroma mixed with the smoky aroma of fried onions and mutton

FLAVOUR PROFILE
Spicy and salty, with a sweet and tangy note of ketchup and an eggy flavour

MOUTHFEEL
Springy, smooth Hokkien noodles with chewy mutton bits and chunky potatoes

For noodles

Water **300 mL**
Salt **3 g / ¹/₂ tsp**
Yellow potatoes, peeled and cut into cubes **150 g**

1. Bring water to a boil. Add salt and potatoes and boil until potatoes are tender. Drain and set aside.

Water **45 g / 3 Tbsp**
Chilli sauce **30 g / 2 Tbsp**
Tomato ketchup **30 g / 2 Tbsp**
Light soya sauce **15 g / 1 Tbsp**
Dark soya sauce **6 g / 1 tsp**

2. Combine ingredients in a bowl. Mix well and set aside.

Corn oil **30 g / 3 Tbsp**
Onion, peeled and sliced **60 g**
Garlic, peeled and minced **20 g / 6 cloves**
Mutton, minced **150 g**
Fresh chilli paste **15 g**
Yellow Hokkien noodles **400 g**
Green peas **80 g**
Bean sprouts **80 g**
Eggs, beaten **110 g / 2**
Tomato, cut into wedges **1**

3. Heat oil in a wok over medium heat and sweat onions until slightly translucent.
4. Add garlic and stir-fry until fragrant.
5. Add mutton and chilli paste and stir-fry until mutton is cooked.
6. Add yellow noodles, green peas and bean sprouts. Stir-fry for 2 minutes and mix well.
7. Push ingredients to side of wok. Add beaten eggs and scramble.
8. Add boiled potatoes, tomato and chilli sauce-tomato ketchup mixture. Mix thoroughly.

For garnishing

Cucumber, sliced **80 g**
Tomato ketchup **60 g**
Fresh green chillies, sliced **25 g**

9. Portion noodles evenly onto serving plates and garnish.
10. Serve hot.

NUTRITION PROFILE	PER SERVING
Energy (kcal)	459
Total fat (g)	19
Saturated fat (g)	4
Cholesterol (mg)	113
Carbohydrate (g)	58
Protein (g)	15
Dietary fibre (g)	2
Sodium (mg)	398

CHEF'S ADVICE

Mutton can be substituted with chicken or pork for a more rounded flavour.

Laksa

Laksa is a spicy noodle dish prepared by the Peranakans who are believed to be Chinese immigrants who settled in the British Settlement and integrated with the local Malayan culture.

The dish is made with thick rice vermicelli mixed with a small amount of green bean vermicelli and bean sprouts in a thick, rich and spicy broth made from chicken and prawn stock cooked with an aromatic spice mix of ground dried red chillies, dried shrimps, shallots, candlenuts, galangal and lemongrass.

A bowl of Nonya laksa is typically served with chicken meat, prawns and fishcake topped up with cucumber slices and finely sliced laksa leaves (*daun kesom*), botanically known as *Persicaria odorata*.

Origins

Laksa is believed to have been created by the Chinese as rice noodles is used for this dish, but research into the origins of the dish are not conclusive. It could also have been created by the Peranakans who were mostly Hokkien Chinese who married local women and integrated with the local Malayan culture.

The word "laksa" may have been derived from the Hindi word, "*lakshah*", the name for a type of noodle. The name is said to be of Sanskrit origin, with links to Indonesia and possible roots in the ancient Majapahit era.

Variations

There are essentially two types of laksa. Laksa *lemak*, with a coconut milk soup base and *assam* laksa, with a clear, sweet, sour and spicy soup base. The sour taste comes from tamarind, known locally as *assam*.

Singapore Laksa

This Peranakan version is rich with seafood such as prawns, fishcakes and dried shrimps. Recent versions include cockles. The dish is served with sambal chilli, laksa leaves and cucumber.

Penang Laksa

This is the most common *assam* version. Its rich flavours are derived from the pungent black prawn paste (*haeko*) mixed with tamarind juice. The fish stock is often made from Indian mackerel and the flavour is enhanced with lemongrass, turmeric, torch ginger flower and shallots. Mint leaves, pineapple and cucumber are used as garnish.

Johore Laksa / Southern Laksa (Laksa Selatan)

The Johore version is made tasty with salted fish and basil, and served with thick rice vermicelli. Condiments and garnishes such as sambal *belacan* (chilli with dried shrimp paste), dried fried grated coconut, basil, lemongrass, cucumber and turnip add a unique Malay flavour.

Sarawak Sambal Laksa

Said to be concocted by Chinese in Sarawak, this version comes with a grey prawn or chicken broth that is not spicy and extremely tasty. It is often served with laksa leaves, lemongrass, coriander, candlenuts, shallots, prawns and shredded fried egg.

SCIENCE CONNECTION

Cockles feed by filtering the plankton in the water. In the process, they accumulate and concentrate microorganisms in their gills and gastrointestinal tract. As such, consuming raw or lightly cooked cockles can cause illness due to the accumulated human pathogenic bacteria and viruses. Heating cockles to 90°C for 90 seconds or simmering them at 70°C for 5 minutes will help to reduce the risk of foodborne illness.

Right: Alternative presentation of laksa — rice noodles with laksa pesto

Laksa

Serves 4

For dried shrimp stock
Dried shrimps **150 g**
Water, warm **250 mL**

1. Place in a bowl and soak for 30 minutes. Strain and reserve stock.

For spice paste
Dried red chillies **25 g**
Shallots, peeled **100 g**
Garlic, peeled **100 g**
Lemongrass, halved **30 g / 2 stalks**
Galangal, peeled and sliced **25 g**
Fresh red chillies **25 g**
Candlenuts **20 g / 10**
Laksa leaves **1 g / 20**
Turmeric, peeled **10 g**
Dried shrimp paste (*belacan*), dry-roasted **20 g**
Corn oil **200 mL**
Water **150 mL**

2. Soak dried red chillies in warm water for 15 minutes.
3. Combine soaked dried shrimps and soaked dried red chillies with the rest of the ingredients in a blender. Blend into a smooth paste.

Corn oil **40 g / 4 Tbsp**

4. Heat oil in a pot over low heat. Add spice paste and fry until it turns deep orange and fragrant.

For gravy
Water **600 mL**
Fresh coconut milk **500 mL**
Fresh grated coconut **20 g**
Sugar **20 g / 1¹/₂ Tbsp**

5. Add ingredients and reserved dried shrimp stock to the pot and bring to a boil.
6. Set gravy aside and keep hot.

To assemble
Thick rice vermicelli (*chor bee hoon*) **400 g**
Fried fishcake, sliced **100 g**
Prawns, peeled and deveined, leaving tails intact **240 g / 12**
Bean sprouts, trimmed **100 g**
Fried bean curd puffs (*tau pok*), sliced **1**
Fresh cockles, shelled **60 g**
Laksa leaves, finely chopped **10 g**

7. Boil a pot of water.
8. Blanch items separately for 15 to 20 seconds.
9. Drain and portion into serving bowls.
10. Ladle gravy over noodles.
11. Garnish with finely chopped laksa leaves.
12. Serve hot.

NUTRITION PROFILE	PER SERVING
Energy (kcal)	1284
Total fat (g)	102
Saturated fat (g)	38
Cholesterol (mg)	206
Carbohydrate (g)	66
Protein (g)	34
Dietary fibre (g)	8
Sodium (mg)	1283

 CHEF'S ADVICE

As an alternative to frying, the spice paste can also be cooked in the microwave oven for 8 minutes.

Mee Rebus

Mee rebus is a dish of noodles in thick gravy. The name of this dish essentially means "boiled noodles", with the word "*mee*" originating from the Hokkien "*mee*" (meaning "noodles") and "*rebus*" being the Malay word for "boiled".

In Singapore, *mee rebus* is generally sold by Malay hawkers and is considered a traditional and heritage Malay dish. Like most hawker fare in Singapore, however, *mee rebus* is actually a fusion (multicultural) dish that features ingredients from various ethnic cultures. For instance, the main component of the dish, noodles, are Chinese, as is the fried bean curd that garnishes the dish.

The gravy is flavoured with Chinese fermented bean paste (*tau cheo*), local krill and/or dried shrimp paste (*belacan*) from the Malays or Kristang (Portuguese-Eurasians). In addition, some recipes also call for lemongrass, galangal and candlenuts which are characteristic of Peranakan cuisine, as well as Indian spices like turmeric and curry powder.

Origins

The use of noodles in *mee rebus* has led to the suggestion that this dish is likely to have originated from the Chinese since noodles are Chinese. It has however also been asserted that *mee rebus* hails from the northern Malaysian states and was brought to Peninsular Malaysia by Indian Muslim traders. It was sold as early as 1918 by itinerant street hawkers from their *kandar* (rattan baskets suspended between a pole). Others concur that the dish is the result of Indian Muslim cooks bringing together Malay and Indian ingredients and cooking techniques. The strong Malay and Chinese influences in this dish may also hint at a Peranakan origin as Peranakan cuisine typically marries Chinese and Malay ingredients and flavours.

Variations and similar dishes

In Singapore, *mee rebus* typically consists of yellow Hokkien noodles covered with a gravy flavoured with dried krill or beef broth and thickened with sweet potatoes or potatoes, garnished with bean spouts, bean curd, hard-boiled egg, fried shallots, coriander, green chillies and calamansi lime.

There is also a vegetarian version of *mee rebus* in which the gravy is made without any meat. Because of the simplicity of this dish, there is a number of noodle dishes that are thought to either have evolved from *mee rebus* or vice versa. These include: *mee jawa*, a Penang specialty with Hokkien noodles; *mee bandung*, a soupy noodle dish with seafood and eggs, which originated in Muar, Malaysia rather than Bandung, Indonesia; the Indonesian *mie celor*, which is very similar to *mee rebus*, with a thick gravy of prawns, coconut milk and flour, and garnished with hard-boiled egg and bean sprouts; and finally, *mee maidin* (or *mee mydin*), a noodle soup with prawns and lettuce.

SCIENCE CONNECTION

Sweet potato is naturally high in starch. It is used in this recipe mainly as a thickener, and also to add colour and flavour to the dish. It is interesting to note that scientists from the US Department of Agriculture have found that the thickening properties of sweet potato is quite similar to that of some starch solutions and are exploring spray-dried sweet potato powder to be used like pre-gelatinised starches.

Right: Alternative presentation of *mee rebus* —
pasta *rebus* with poached egg

Mee Rebus

Serves 4

For spice paste
Yellow onion, peeled **60 g**
Garlic, peeled **25 g**
Galangal, peeled **15 g**
Ginger, peeled **4 g**
Dried shrimp paste (*belacan*), dry-roasted **8 g**
Water **45 g / 3 Tbsp**

1. Combine ingredients in a blender and blend into a fine paste.

Dried shrimps **15 g**

2. Soak dried shrimps in warm water for 30 minutes. Drain and finely chop soaked dried shrimps. Set aside.

Corn oil **30 g / 3 Tbsp**
Fermented bean paste (*tau cheo*) **75 g**
Curry powder **15 g / 3 tsp**
Coriander powder **6 g / 1^1/$_2$ tsp**
Chilli powder **3 g / ^{3}/$_4$ tsp**

3. Heat oil in a pot over low heat and fry spice paste until fragrant.
4. Add chopped dried shrimps, fermented bean paste and powdered spices. Continue to fry until fragrant. Set aside.

For gravy
Orange sweet potatoes, peeled and diced **300 g**

5. Boil sweet potatoes until soft. Drain and mash well. Set aside.

Water **750 mL**
Sugar **60 g / 3^3/$_4$ Tbsp**
Salt **4 g / ^{3}/$_4$ tsp**

6. Combine spice paste and mashed sweet potatoes in a large pot over low heat. Mix thoroughly.
7. Add water gradually and mix into the sweet potato paste, stirring continuously with a whisk. Season with sugar and salt.
8. Simmer for 10 minutes. Set aside and keep hot.

For noodles
Yellow Hokkien noodles **400 g**
Bean sprouts **50 g**

9. Boil a pot of water and blanch ingredients separately for 15 to 20 seconds.
10. Portion equally into serving bowls.
11. Ladle equal amounts of gravy over noodles and bean sprouts.

For garnishing
Eggs, hard-boiled and halved **2**
Fried shallots **50 g**
Chinese celery, chopped **10 g**
Firm bean curd (*tau kua*), diced and fried **200 g**
Fresh green chillies, sliced **25 g**
Calamansi limes, halved **2**

12. Garnish with remaining ingredients.
13. Serve hot.

NUTRITION PROFILE	PER SERVING
Energy (kcal)	476
Total fat (g)	17
Saturated fat (g)	4
Cholesterol (mg)	101
Carbohydrate (g)	70
Protein (g)	12
Dietary fibre (g)	3
Sodium (mg)	589

CHEF'S ADVICE

To thicken the gravy further, make a cornflour slurry and add while stirring until the desired consistency is achieved.

Mee Siam

Mee siam is a dish of rice vermicelli bathed in a sweet and tangy gravy. The rice vermicelli is stir-fried in an aromatic mix of shallots, dried red chillies and dried shrimp paste (*belacan*), and served with prawns, firm bean curd (*tau kua*) and bean sprouts.

The gravy is made from fermented soya beans (*tau cheo*), shallots, dried red chillies and tamarind juice. For those who want to spice up the dish, a dollop of sambal can be added.

Origins

Mee siam, as the name suggests, means Siamese noodles. The late Mrs Lee Chin Koon, a well-known Nonya cook, identified *mee siam* as originating from Thailand. The three flavours of *mee siam* — hot, sweet and sour — are basic flavours of Thai cuisine.

Similar Thai dishes include *mee kati* (noodles with coconut milk), *kanom jeen nam-prik* (spicy rice noodles) and *pad thai* (fried rice noodles with tamarind sauce).

However, amongst local food writers and critics, there is dispute over whether *mee siam* is of Malay origin or an innovation of the Peranakans. One critic claims that the dish is a perfect example of Singapore hawker food, with a mix of flavours from Chinese, Malay Peranakan and Thai cuisines. Wendy Hutton, another well-known food author, believes the dish comes from Penang, where Thai influences on local cooking are common.

Variations

In Singapore, there are Chinese, Malay and Indian versions of the dish. In the Chinese version, the main item is rice vermicelli which is fried in a chilli paste mixed with ground dried shrimps. The dish is topped with prawns, fishcake slices and thinly-sliced omelette.

The Malay version of the dish is topped with sliced hard-boiled egg and Chinese chives, and is often served without the coconut gravy.

The Indian version comes with a coconut gravy that is lighter in colour, sweeter and less sourish than the other versions.

In Malaysia, *mee siam* is generally fried and served dry.

SCIENCE CONNECTION

Rice vermicelli has a low glycemic index (GI) and it is generally lower compared to the white rice from which it is made. This is due to the processing method used in the manufacture of rice vermicelli which results in the formation of a type of starch that is resistant to digestion by alpha-amylase in the small intestine. A large body of evidence now suggests that the consumption of low GI foods may be beneficial for the management of chronic diseases such as diabetes.

Right: Alternative presentation of *mee siam* — *mee siam* salad with tamarind vinaigrette

Mee Siam

Serves 4

For spice paste
Dried red chillies **8 g**
Dried shrimps **50 g**

1. Soak ingredients for 15 minutes. Drain and set aside.

Shallots, peeled **80 g**
Garlic, peeled **20 g**
Candlenuts **20 g / 10**
Corn oil **30 g / 3 Tbsp**
Water **30 g / 2 Tbsp**
Dried shrimp paste (*belacan*), dry-roasted **5 g**

2. Combine soaked dried chillies and dried shrimps with the rest of the ingredients in a blender and blend into a fine paste.

Corn oil **30 g / 3 Tbsp**

3. Heat oil in a medium pot and fry spice paste until it turns deep orange and fragrant.

Fermented bean paste (*tau cheo*) **100 g**
Sugar **100 g**

4. Add ingredients to the pot and stir until sugar dissolves.
5. Remove from heat and split paste into 2 equal portions. Set aside.

For gravy
Water **45 g / 3 Tbsp**
Tamarind pulp **60 g**

6. Combine ingredients and mix well. Strain to obtain 60 g tamarind juice. Set aside.

Water **600 mL**

7. In another pot, combine first portion of cooked spice paste and water. Bring to a boil.
8. Add tamarind juice and mix well.
9. Set gravy aside and keep hot.

For noodles
Corn oil **30 g / 3 Tbsp**
Bean sprouts **100 g**
Water **30 g / 2 Tbsp**

10. Heat oil in a wok over medium heat. Add second portion of cooked spice paste with remaining ingredients.

Dried rice vermicelli (*bee hoon*), soaked in cool water **300 g**

11. Add noodles and toss well for 2 minutes or until noodles are well coated with spice paste.

For garnishing

Medium-size prawns, peeled, leaving tails intact, cooked **8**
Eggs, hard-boiled and halved **2**
Firm bean curd (*tau kua*), diced and deep-fried **50 g**
Chinese chives, cut into 2-cm lengths **40 g**
Calamansi limes, halved **2**
Fresh green chillies, sliced **25 g**

12. Portion noodles evenly onto serving plates and ladle hot gravy over.
13. Top with garnishing ingredients.
14. Serve hot.

NUTRITION PROFILE	PER SERVING
Energy (kcal)	479
Total fat (g)	24
Saturated fat (g)	4
Cholesterol (mg)	209
Carbohydrate (g)	45
Protein (g)	24
Dietary fibre (g)	3
Sodium (mg)	661

 CHEF'S ADVICE

Do not overcook the hard-boiled eggs as it will form a grayish ring around the yolks.

Meat and Seafood

Chilli Crab • 63

Fish Head Curry • 69

Orh Luak • 75

Otak Otak • 81

Satay with Peanut Sauce • 87

Teochew Bak Kut Teh • 93

Chilli Crab

Chilli crab is noted as an authentic Singaporean dish with a multicultural flavour, combining Asian flavours of garlic, ginger and chillies with Western tomato ketchup in the recipe.

Chilli crab first appeared in Singapore in the 1950s and today the dish is available on the menus of most local seafood restaurants, hawker centres and *zhi char* (or cooked-to-order) food stalls.

Singapore has many versions of chilli crab; some with a sambal-like sauce, others heavier on the ketchup, and versions rich with beaten eggs.

The birthplace of chilli crab is said to be the Bedok kampong in the eastern part of Singapore. Back in the 1950s, seafood was plentiful at the beaches off Bedok.

It was thought that a Mr Lim Choon Ngee, a policeman by profession and weekend fisherman, would bring his catch home to his wife, Mdm Cher Yam Tian, to cook. On one occasion, Mr Lim suggested that Mdm Cher add bottled chilli sauce to her dish of stir-fried crabs which she would normally prepare using tomato sauce. The resulting dish was so tasty that the couple began selling it from a pushcart at Bedok corner. The set up back then was just basic wooden tables and low stools, and cooking was done over an open fire.

Chilli crab is a dish of crabs stir-fried in chilli sauce and tomato ketchup gravy, finished with egg white and cornflour. Mud crabs from Indonesia, Sri Lanka, Vietnam and the Philippines are normally used. Bread is typically served with the dish for mopping up the spicy and sour gravy. In recent years, baguette or fried steamed Chinese buns (*mantou*) often accompany the dish.

Variations and similar dishes
The popularity of chilli crab has prompted variations to the dish such as black pepper crab, butter crab and salted egg cream crab.

The Singapore Tourism Board officially promotes chilli crab as one of Singapore's signature dishes through its websites and overseas events. It is common to find chilli crab on the menus of overseas restaurants that offer Singapore cuisine.

SCIENCE CONNECTION

Have you ever wondered why crabs turn from a blue-green or brown colour to a bright orange-red colour after cooking? This is because the crab shell contains a group of carotenoid pigments known as astaxanthin, which are orange-red in colour. In live crabs, these pigments attach themselves to the protein molecules, creating the crab's blue-green or brown colour. This helps the crabs camouflage themselves at the bottom of the sea. During cooking, the heat changes the protein structures, exposing the astaxanthin and other carotenoid pigments that are heat stable. This results in the crabs becoming bright orange-red upon cooking.

Right: Alternative presentation of chilli crab — chilli crab ravioli in tangy tomato and chilli sauce

Chilli Crab

Serves 4

Mud crabs **1.2 kg**

1. Freeze crabs for 20 to 30 minutes. Scrub crabs clean, then pull off top shells.
2. Chop off pincers and crack lightly. Cut crabs in half and trim legs. Pull off and discard gills. Rinse well. Set aside.

For spice paste
Corn oil **40 g / 4 Tbsp**
Fresh red chillies, seeded **140 g**
Red onion, peeled **100 g**
Garlic, peeled **40 g**
Ginger, peeled **30 g**
Bird's eye chillies (*cili padi*) **5 g**

3. Combine ingredients in a blender and blend into a fine paste. Set aside.

Corn oil **70 g / 7 Tbsp**

4. Heat oil in a wok over low heat and stir-fry spice paste until it turns deep red and fragrant.
5. Add crab pieces and stir-fry for 2 minutes until crab shells turn orange.

For sauce
Tomato ketchup **100 g**
Sugar **45 g / 3 Tbsp**
Salt **3 g / $^1/_2$ tsp**
Chicken seasoning powder
  10 g / 2$^1/_2$ tsp
Water **500 mL**

6. Add ingredients to wok and mix well. Simmer over low heat for 5 minutes.

Cornflour **12 g / 1 Tbsp**
Water **15 g / 1 Tbsp**

7. Combine to form a slurry.
8. Bring crab mixture to a boil and add cornflour slurry to thicken gravy.

Eggs, beaten **110 g / 2**

9. Drizzle beaten eggs evenly over sauce and leave for 5 seconds before stirring to create egg ribbons.
10. Dish out and serve hot.

NUTRITION PROFILE	PER SERVING
Energy (kcal)	622
Total fat (g)	44
Saturated fat (g)	7
Cholesterol (mg)	181
Carbohydrate (g)	30
Protein (g)	23
Dietary fibre (g)	1
Sodium (mg)	1266

CHEF'S ADVICE

Before adding the crabs to the cooked spice paste, blanch them in hot oil to develop more flavour and keep the flesh together.

Fish Head Curry

In the local mindset, curry and spices are closely connected to Indian culture, and by extension, the famously tangy curry fish head dish is often thought to have originated from the Indian subcontinent.

However, it may surprise many that while fish curry is found in India, fish head curry is not a typical Indian dish at all. Fish head curry was actually created in Singapore in the 1950s by an Indian man, Mr M.J. Gomez. Mr Gomez noticed that the Chinese enjoyed eating large fish heads, so he experimented and mixed Kerala-style curry with the head of the red/golden snapper to create the now famous dish.

Curry fish head soon became popular among the Chinese, Indian and Malay communities, so much so that in the 1970s and 1980s, stalls took to advertising their own "Gomez Fish Head Curry" or "Original Gomez Curry". By 1983, the fish head curry craze was widespread and the now defunct newspaper, the *Singapore Monitor* noted that the popularity of the dish also led to the increase in price of fish heads in Singapore.

Variations and similar dishes
The classic fish head curry combines Kerala-style curry with okra (ladies' fingers), brinjals, tamarind juice (for the signature tangy flavour) and coconut milk with the head of the red or golden snapper. The dish is served bubbling hot in a clay pot to preserve the heat, and is eaten with rice, buns or pappadams, which are slathered or dipped in the curry before consuming.

The Chinese version is mostly similar to the classic dish, except that the curry is not as thick or spicy. This variant relies on the tamarind juice for flavour.

The Nonya version features a rich, spicy curry with a tangy flavour from the use of dried sour fruit slices (*assam gelugor*) or lime juice.

SCIENCE CONNECTION
An interesting fact about okra is its slimy mucilage made up of carbohydrate compounds (called polysaccharides), small amounts of protein and trace minerals. Mucilage, which is also found in cacti and aloe vera, increases the water-holding capacity of plants. In cooking, vegetables with mucilage can help thicken gravies and soups. Thus, adding more okra to a curry will make the gravy thicker.

Right: Alternative presentation of fish head curry — baked curry fish rice with okra and pappadam

Fish Head Curry

Serves 4

AROMA
Fragrant blend of spices and herbs with a subtle aroma of curry leaves

FLAVOUR PROFILE
Spicy and savoury with a hint of tangy tamarind against a slightly creamy coconut flavour

MOUTHFEEL
Thickened curry of ground spices with tender vegetable chunks and firm-fleshed fish

For spice paste
Cumin seeds **5 g / 2 tsp**
Fennel seeds **5 g / 2 tsp**
Fenugreek seeds **2.5 g / 1 tsp**
Black mustard seeds **2 g / ¹/₂ tsp**

1. Heat a pan and dry-fry seeds until fragrant and mustard seeds pop.
2. Combine in a blender and grind until fine. Set aside.

Dried red chillies **10 g**
Fresh red chillies **30 g**
Garlic, peeled **30 g**
Shallots, peeled **25 g**
Galangal, peeled **10 g**
Coriander powder **12 g / 1 Tbsp**
Turmeric powder **8 g / 2 tsp**
Chilli powder **4 g / 1 tsp**
Corn oil **60 g / 6 Tbsp**

3. Soak dried red chillies in warm water for 15 minutes. Drain.
4. Combine soaked dried red chillies with the rest of the ingredients in a blender and blend into a fine paste.

Corn oil **20 g / 2 Tbsp**

5. Heat oil a large pan over low heat and add chilli paste and ground seeds.
6. Stir constantly for 10 minutes until oil separates and paste darkens. Set aside.

For curry
Large red/golden snapper fish head **600 g / 1**
Salt **50 g**

7. Rinse fish head well and season with salt. Set aside for 5 minutes before rinsing away salt.

Brinjal, halved lengthwise and cut at an angle into 3-cm sections **100 g**
Okra, cut at an angle into 3-cm sections **60 g**

8. Place vegetables and fish head in a large heatproof tray and steam for 10 minutes. Set aside.

Corn oil **20 g / 2 Tbsp**
Onion, peeled, finely chopped **70 g**
Lemongrass, bruised **30 g / 2 stalks**
Curry leaves **15 g**
Ginger, peeled and sliced **30 g**
Water **400 mL**

9. Heat oil in a large pot and sweat onion until light brown.
10. Add spice paste, lemongrass, curry leaves and ginger and stir-fry for 5 minutes until fragrant.
11. Add water and simmer for 10 minutes.

Tamarind pulp **60 g**
Water **45 g / 3 Tbsp**
Tomato, quartered **90 g / 1**

12. Combine tamarind pulp with water and mix well. Strain to obtain 60 g tamarind juice.
13. Add tamarind juice and tomato quarters to the pot and mix well.
14. Simmer for another 5 minutes.

Coconut milk **50 g / 3¹/₂ Tbsp**
Sugar **15 g / 1 Tbsp**
Salt **8 g / 1¹/₂ tsp**

15. Add coconut milk and mix well.
16. Add partially cooked fish head and vegetables and bring to a boil.
17. Season to taste and serve hot.

NUTRITION PROFILE	PER SERVING
Energy (kcal)	478
Total fat (g)	35
Saturated fat (g)	8
Cholesterol (mg)	39
Carbohydrate (g)	23
Protein (g)	18
Dietary fibre (g)	4
Sodium (mg)	1840

 CHEF'S ADVICE

To avoid a fishy flavour in the sauce, clean the fish head well and make sure it is free of any impurities such as blood or blood clots.

Orh Luak

Early migrants from Chaozhou and Fujian province in China introduced *orh luak* (oyster omelette) to the locals, and the dish was gradually modified with the use of limes and chillies to suit the taste preferences of the locals.

Oyster, a family of the shellfish, thrives along the shallow rocky coastlines of Fujian province by the South China Sea. It is a staple among the Teochew community living there, and one of the key dishes that the Teochews prepare using oysters is *orh luak*.

Today, *orh luak* is found wherever there is a Teochew community — in Taiwan, Singapore, Malaysia, Indonesia and even the Philippines.

Variations and similar dishes
Variations of the dish can be found in the southern regions of China and depending on regional variations, a savoury sauce may be poured on top of the omelette for added taste.

Two variations of the dish can be found in Singapore, one being *orh luak* which is also called *orh jian* (fried oysters) and the other *orh nerng* (fried egg).

Orh luak or *orh jian* is made by adding a starch batter to a hot pan with a good amount of oil, followed by eggs and a dash of fish sauce. Using the right cooking temperature and type of starch will ensure that the *orh luak* has a crispy omelette with gooey bits of starch within or a sticky omelette with little crispy bits embedded in the omelette.

Orh nerng is made primarily of eggs, with less starch, for those who enjoy the taste of fluffy, tender eggs with the oysters.

SCIENCE CONNECTION

In this recipe, a combination of five types of flour is used to give the oyster omelette its unique flavour and texture. Tapioca flour and sweet potato flour are root starches with large granule size, and contain more amylopectin (one of the two components of starch). This makes them excellent thickeners for the omelette batter. In addition, when they are mixed with water and heated, they undergo a process called gelatinisation and become translucent. This gives the omelette a chewy texture and attractive appearance.

Rice flour and mung bean flour are cereal starches with a smaller granule size, contributing to their finer texture. They impart a distinct aroma to the omelette.

Plain flour contains gluten protein that forms a gluten network upon kneading, providing structure to the omelette when the batter is cooked.

Right: Alternative presentation of *orh luak* — oyster *tako* ball with Thai chilli sauce

Orh Luak

Serves 4

Water **600 mL**
Tapioca flour **120 g**
Rice flour **60 g**
Plain flour **30 g**
Mung bean flour **30 g**
Sweet potato flour **15 g**

1. Combine ingredients and mix well into a smooth batter.

Corn oil **40 g / 4 Tbsp**
Eggs, beaten **220 g / 4**
Fresh oysters **200 g**
Fish sauce **15 g / 1 Tbsp**
Spring onion, chopped **16 g / 2 sprigs**
Coriander leaves **14 g / 2 sprigs**

2. Heat half the oil in a large pan over high heat.
3. Ladle in adequate amount of batter to thinly coat pan. Let batter cook until crispy.
4. Add adequate amount of eggs and oysters. Spread evenly.
5. Season with fish sauce and flip omelette.
6. Allow batter to cook.
7. Add a handful of spring onion and coriander and remove to a serving plate.

For chilli dip
Rice vinegar **36 g / 3 Tbsp**
Sugar **5 g / 1 tsp**
Salt **3 g / 1/2 tsp**
Garlic, peeled **30 g**
Fresh red chillies, seeded **60 g**
Water **45 g / 3 Tbsp**

8. Combine ingredients in a blender and blend well. Set aside.

9. Repeat steps 2 to 7 until ingredients are used up.
10. Serve hot with chilli dip on the side.

NUTRITION PROFILE	PER SERVING
Energy (kcal)	460
Total fat (g)	21
Saturated fat (g)	4
Cholesterol (mg)	181
Carbohydrate (g)	57
Protein (g)	11
Dietary fibre (g)	1
Sodium (mg)	518

 CHEF'S ADVICE
For a crisp omelette, ensure that the batter is thinly spread out and just coats the surface of the frying pan.

Otak Otak

Otak otak is a grilled fishcake made of ground fish meat blended with coconut milk, eggs and spices. It can be found in Indonesia, Malaysia and Singapore.

In Singapore and Malaysia, *otak otak* is traditionally wrapped in coconut leaves. In Indonesia, it is wrapped in banana leaves. Wrapping the fish paste in coconut or banana leaves helps prevent the parcels from burning when they are grilled, and infuses them with a distinct smoky aroma from the charcoal fire.

Otak otak is often served as accompaniment to *nasi lemak* a popular Malay rice dish cooked with coconut milk. It is also a favourite snack eaten on its own or used as a sandwich filling. Modern day demand has made *otak otak* available in supermarkets as a frozen food item.

Origins

Otak is the Malay word for brains, and it has been said that the dish got its name because the blended fish paste resembles brains.

Otak otak from Indonesia is whitish in colour, while the *otak otak* from Malaysia and Singapore is reddish-orange or brown due to the use of chilli, turmeric and curry powder.

Variations

Otak otak is most commonly made using the flesh of the Spanish mackerel (*ikan tenggiri*), but there are also variations made using fish heads, prawns, cuttlefish and crab. There are different recipes originating from different regions as well.

In Indonesia, *otak otak* is commonly associated with Palembang, South Sumatra, but it is also very popular in Jakarta and Makassar. In Palembang, *otak otak* is eaten with *cuko* (a sweet, sour and spicy vinegar sauce), and in Jakarta, it is enjoyed with a spicy peanut sauce.

The *otak otak* from Muar in the south of Malaysia is particularly renowned as it is made from freshly caught Spanish mackerel from the Muar river.

Nonya *otak otak* comes from the northern Malaysian state of Penang where it wrapped in banana leaves and steamed.

SCIENCE CONNECTION

Spices are used in cooking to add flavour, colour and aroma to food. Grinding spices helps to unlock their natural flavours and provide uniformity and intensity of flavour. Spices contain both volatile and non-volatile oils that are responsible for imparting flavour. When the plant tissues are damaged through blending, the flavouring compounds that are soluble in oil will be released when the spice paste is stir-fried in oil. To intensify the flavour and aroma of the spices, the spice paste can be cooked until it is dry.

Right: Alternative presentation of *otak otak* — *otak otak* on sticky rice with *nam prik* sauce

Otak Otak

Serves 4

For fish paste
Spanish mackerel flesh **75 g**
Water **30 g / 2 Tbsp**

1. Combine in a blender and blend into a smooth paste. Set aside.

For spice paste
Dried red chillies **10 g**
Fresh red chillies, seeded **50 g**
Bird's eye chilli (*cili padi*) **5 g**
Shallots, peeled **20 g**
Garlic, peeled **10 g**
Galangal, peeled **10 g**
Turmeric powder **2 g / $1/2$ tsp**
Lemongrass, bruised **5 g**
Dried shrimp paste (*belacan*), dry-roasted **3 g**
Candlenuts **10 g / 5**
Corn oil **40 g / 4 Tbsp**

2. Soak dried red chillies in warm water for 15 minutes. Drain.
3. Combine soaked dried red chillies with the rest of the ingredients in a blender and blend into a fine paste.

For *otak otak* paste
Coconut milk **65 g / 4 Tbsp**
Kaffir lime leaves, finely sliced **2**
Egg, beaten **45 g**
Cornflour **24 g / 2 Tbsp**
Salt **5 g / 1 tsp**
Sugar **5 g / 1 tsp**

4. In a large mixing bowl, combine ingredients with fish and spice pastes. Mix well.

Spanish mackerel flesh, diced **75 g**

5. Fold in diced fish.

To assemble
Banana leaves, cut into rectangular sheets, each 20-cm x 15-cm **12 sheets**
Corn oil **as needed**
Toothpicks **24**

6. In a frying pan, lightly toast leaves on both sides, then brush the inner surface with a little oil.
7. Spoon 60 g paste on the oiled leaf and fold longer sides of leaf over to enclose filling. Seal open ends with toothpicks.
8. Repeat until ingredients are used up.
9. Grill or bake at 180°C for 7 minutes. Pierce the middle of a parcel with a toothpick to check for doneness. The toothpick should come out clean.
10. Serve hot.

NUTRITION PROFILE	PER SERVING (3 pieces)
Energy (kcal)	370
Total fat (g)	28
Saturated fat (g)	8
Cholesterol (mg)	70
Carbohydrate (g)	14
Protein (g)	13
Dietary fibre (g)	2
Sodium (mg)	583

CHEF'S ADVICE

To give the fish paste a firmer texture, throw it against the bowl repeatedly until the paste is of the desired consistency.

Satay with Peanut Sauce

Satay is a popular dish of grilled meat on skewers. It is typically served with a peanut dipping sauce, *ketupat* (glutinous rice cakes cooked in woven coconut leaf cases) and slices of raw cucumber and onion.

Satay (spelt *sate* in Malay and Bahasa Indonesia) is sold by Chinese, Malay and Indian Muslim vendors. Similar to shashlik and shish kebab, satay consists of bite-size (or sometimes minced) pieces of marinated meat such as beef, chicken, mutton and pork skewered on thick bamboo sticks and cooked over a charcoal (or, these days, electric) grill. The meat marinade is a concoction of spices and aromatics such as ground coriander seeds, turmeric powder, galangal, lemongrass, shallots, candlenut and garlic, seasoned with sugar and salt.

Origins
Satay is thought to have originated in Java, Indonesia, and brought to Singapore by Muslim traders. Another theory proposes that during the colonial period, Indonesian cooks, not wanting to waste the fatty scraps of meat their European masters rejected, skewered them on leaf stalks to cook over fire.

As for the name, sources suggest that it came from the word *sathai* (with reference to skin or surface meat, from an unspecified Indian language) or from the Hokkien phrase, *sar teh,* meaning "three pieces".

Variations and similar dishes
Satay is served with a thick peanut sauce flavoured with spices and thickened with ground peanuts. The sauce is rich, slightly sweet and slightly spicy. Malay satay sauce includes *kecap manis* (a sweet dark soya sauce), while Chinese (specifically Hainanese) satay sauce sometimes includes pineapple purée to sweeten the sauce.

Chinese and Nonya satay vendors in Singapore usually offer a choice of chicken, pork and mutton satay, and the meat may be marinated Chinese-style, using Chinese five-spice powder and lemongrass. Malay satay vendors will offer chicken, beef, mutton and sometimes offal like liver, tripe and lung.

SCIENCE CONNECTION

Meat is a very nutritious medium for the growth of microorganisms, some of which can cause food spoilage or foodborne illnesses if allowed to proliferate. Therefore, it is important to keep raw meat refrigerated (between 0°C and 3°C) when marinating to contain the growth of microorganisms. If there is cooked food in the refrigerator, avoid cross-contamination by covering the raw meat and keeping it below the cooked food.

Before the invention of refrigeration, meat was preserved using spices or by drying and curing it. It is now known that spices such as garlic contain antimicrobial compounds that help prevent or delay the spoilage of food by disrupting bacterial cell membrane functions and inhibiting their growth.

Right: Alternative presentation of satay with peanut sauce
— savoury chicken satay pie

Satay with Peanut Sauce

Makes 36 pieces (approximately 25 g per piece)

Bamboo skewers **36 sticks**

1. Soak in water for 1 hour. Drain and set aside.

Corn oil **40 g / 4 Tbsp**
Kecap manis (sweet dark soya sauce) **75 g / 5 Tbsp**
Shallots, peeled **60 g**
Lemongrass, thinly sliced **10 g**
Garlic, peeled **10 g**

2. Combine ingredients in a blender and blend into a paste.

Coriander powder **4 g / 1 tsp**
Turmeric powder **8 g / 2 tsp**
Chilli powder **4 g / 1 tsp**
Cumin powder **4 g / 1 tsp**
Fennel powder **5 g / 1 tsp**
Salt **3 g / ¹/₂ tsp**

3. Add powdered spices and salt. Continue to blend into a fine paste.
4. Transfer to a bowl.

Chicken thigh, boneless **500 g**

5. Remove skin from chicken and cut into 2-cm cubes. Place in a big bowl and mix well with the paste.
6. Cover and refrigerate for at least 10 hours or overnight.
7. Thread 25 g of marinated chicken onto each bamboo skewer and set aside.
8. Repeat step 7 for remaining chicken.
9. Grill skewers over a charcoal grill. Turn skewers frequently to prevent burning.

For peanut sauce
Dried red chillies **10 g**
Shallots, peeled **50 g**
Lemongrass, thinly sliced **5 g**
Garlic, peeled **10 g**
Galangal, peeled and sliced **5 g**
Coriander powder **12 g / 1 Tbsp**
Corn oil **30 g / 3 Tbsp**

10. Soak dried red chillies in warm water for 15 minutes. Drain.
11. Combine soaked dried red chillies with the rest of the ingredients in a blender and blend into a fine paste.

Tamarind pulp **10 g**
Water **5 g**

12. Combine tamarind pulp with water and mix well. Strain to obtain 5 g tamarind juice.

Water **220 mL**
Peanuts, ground **100 g**
Brown sugar **60 g**
Lime juice **15 g / 1 Tbsp**
Salt **3 g / ¹/₂ tsp**

13. Heat a pot over low heat and fry the paste until it turns deep red and fragrant.
14. Add tamarind juice and remaining ingredients. Mix well.
15. Simmer sauce over low heat for 5 minutes.
16. Serve chicken satay and peanut sauce hot.

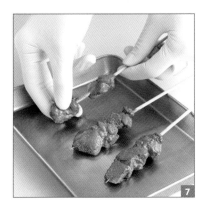

NUTRITION PROFILE	PER SERVING (6 pieces)
Energy (kcal)	407
Total fat (g)	24
Saturated fat (g)	5
Cholesterol (mg)	122
Carbohydrate (g)	24
Protein (g)	26
Dietary fibre (g)	3
Sodium (mg)	660

CHEF'S ADVICE

If a charcoal grill is unavailable, the satay can also be baked for about 10 minutes in an oven preheated to 180°C.

Teochew Bak Kut Teh

Bak kut teh translates into Mandarin as "*rou gu cha*", meaning "meat bone tea". This dish was introduced by the coolies from Fujian province, southern China in the 19th century.

These coolies worked as labourers at the port, carrying goods from the ships for a few cents based on the weight of the goods they carried. At the end of each long day, they would boil pork ribs and intestines with strong Chinese medicinal herbs and spices (including star anise, cinnamon, cloves, Chinese angelica and garlic) to flavour the soup, and to replenish their energy. Pork ribs and intestines, being the cheaper parts were what the coolies could afford, paired with a bowl of rice and brewed Chinese tea.

Variations

Hokkien/Fujian Bak Kut Teh

Hokkien/Fujian *bak kut teh* is generally darker in colour as it is prepared using herbs, spices and a mixture of light and dark soya sauces. It was sold in the Hokkien Street area where many Hokkiens lived in the 1950s.

Teochew Bak Kut Teh

Teochew *bak kut teh* was sold in the Clarke Quay and River Valley areas after World War II, where there was a large threshold of Teochew and Hokkien labourers. The soup was made by boiling pork bones with garlic and pepper. This Teochew version is popularly found in Singapore today.

SCIENCE CONNECTION

One of the reasons for adding pork bones to *bak kut teh* stock is to contribute "body" or richness to the stock. When sufficient pork bones and meat are added, gel formation may be observed when the stock is chilled. Gelatin, the protein derived from collagen in bones and meat, is responsible for this thermo-reversible reaction. When gelatin is dispersed in hot water, it forms a sol, which is free to flow. Upon cooling, it thickens as the gelatin molecules bond and form a 3D continuous network, trapping water inside.

Right: Alternative presentation of *bak kut teh* — *bak kut teh* consommé with dough fritters

Teochew Bak Kut Teh

Serves 4

Pork ribs **1 kg**
Pork bones **500 g**

1. Chop pork ribs and bones into 8-cm pieces.
2. Boil a pot of water and blanch pork ribs and bones to remove any impurities.
3. Drain and rinse with cold water.

Water **3 L**
Whole garlic, unpeeled **250 g**
Whole white peppercorns, toasted **45 g**
Dried Chinese mushrooms, soaked (optional) **20 g**

4. Place ingredients in a large pot with pork ribs and pork bones. Bring to a boil.
5. Lower heat, cover and simmer for 1$\frac{1}{2}$ hours.
6. Skim off any residue if necessary.

Salt **10 g / 2 tsp**
Coriander leaves **15 g / 2 sprigs**
Fresh red chillies, sliced **50 g**
Dark soya sauce **18 g / 1 Tbsp**

7. Season with salt and portion equally into serving bowls.
8. Garnish with coriander leaves.
9. Serve hot with sliced red chillies and dark soya sauce.

NUTRITION PROFILE	PER SERVING
Energy (kcal)	333
Total fat (g)	20
Saturated fat (g)	7
Cholesterol (mg)	95
Carbohydrate (g)	5
Protein (g)	33
Dietary fibre (g)	<1
Sodium (mg)	1461

CHEF'S ADVICE

For a more robust flavour, add oyster sauce and Chinese herbs such as star anise and cinnamon.

Light Meals and Snacks

Black Carrot Cake

Fried carrot cake, or *chye tow kway* in the Teochew dialect, is a dish of carrot cake stir-fried with garlic, eggs and preserved radish.

There are two versions to the dish, a white version, which is cooked with light soya sauce, and a black version, which is cooked with sweet dark soya sauce. Modern versions may have fresh prawns and chilli paste added to enhance the flavour of the dish. Both versions can be found at hawker centres, and dim sum restaurants may also have the dishes on their menus.

The carrot cake is made by steaming a mixture of rice flour, water and shredded Chinese white radish (also known as white carrot). The steamed cake is then cooled and cut into small cubes for frying.

Origins

The origins of carrot cake can be traced to Chaoshan province in southern China where it was known as *mi gao* (rice cake) or *koh gao* (starch cake). The basic dough was made simply from rice flour without radish. After steaming, the dough was cut into small cubes and fried with garlic, chopped spring onion and soya sauce.

Introduced in the early 1960s into Singapore and Malaysia by Teochew immigrants, the dish was cooked with dark soya sauce and known as *char kway* (fried rice cake).

Variations

In dim sum restaurants, the steamed carrot cake is typically cut into small rectangular slabs, then served as it is or pan-fried for a crisp outer layer. Some restaurants may also mill the rice grains instead of using commercial rice flour, so the carrot cake has a soft and melting texture.

In Malaysia, hawkers in Penang sell a version called *char kway kak* (Hokkien for fried cake). The rice cake is made purely from rice flour without the Chinese white radish, and the dish is topped with prawns and cockles. In night markets in Johor, it is common to see the white version of *chye tow kway* fried with Chinese sausages, chopped barbecued pork (*char siew*) and bean sprouts.

SCIENCE CONNECTION

The white radish used in this recipe belongs to the botanical family, *Cruciferae*. It was introduced to Japan from China about 1,000 years ago. This brassica vegetable is cultivated for its root and, in some countries, the leaves are also eaten as a vegetable. The roots are harvested when still crisp and can be eaten raw for a pungent mustard taste or cooked. The pungency in radish is attributed to the phytochemical 4-methylthio-3-butenyl isothiocyanate which is produced when the tissues in the plant are bruised, such as during shredding. If the pungency is not desired in the final dish, it can be removed by blanching the shredded radish in boiling water for a few minutes and draining it well before use.

Right: Alternative presentation of black carrot cake — steamed savoury carrot gateau with braised preserved radish and caramelised dark soya sauce

Black Carrot Cake

Serves 4

Water **500 mL**
Rice flour **130 g**
Cornflour **12 g / 1 Tbsp**
Wheat starch **12 g / 1 Tbsp**

1. Combine ingredients and mix until smooth. Set aside.

Chinese white radish, peeled **400 g**

2. Shred radish into thin strips.

Corn oil **20 g / 2 Tbsp**
Preserved salted radish (*xian chye poh*), rinsed **30 g**

3. Heat oil in a pan over low heat and stir-fry preserved radish until fragrant.
4. Add shredded radish and mix well. Cook for 5 minutes until radish turns translucent.

Water **280 mL**
Sugar **5 g / 1 tsp**
White pepper powder **2 g / ¹/₂ tsp**

5. Add ingredients to pan and cook for 5 minutes.
6. Turn off heat and pour in flour mixture.
7. Stir continuously for 2 minutes until it becomes a thick paste.
8. Transfer mixture to a greased 30-cm x 15-cm x 5-cm pan. Cover with plastic wrap and steam for 1 hour.
9. Set aside to cool to room temperature. Unmould and cut into rectangular pieces.

Corn oil **60 g / 3 Tbsp**
Garlic, peeled and minced **10 g**
Eggs, beaten **220 g / 4**

10. Heat oil in a pan over medium heat and fry garlic until fragrant.
11. Add sliced carrot cake and stir-fry over high heat until lightly brown.
12. Add beaten eggs and scramble for 1 minute.

Sweet black sauce **75 g / 4 Tbsp**
Fish sauce **30 g / 2 Tbsp**
Dark soya sauce **35 g / 2 Tbsp**

13. Combine in a small bowl. Add to pan.

Spring onion, sliced **1 sprig**

14. Turn off heat and add spring onion. Mix well and portion evenly onto serving plates.
15. Serve hot.

NUTRITION PROFILE	PER SERVING
Energy (kcal)	608
Total fat (g)	35
Saturated fat (g)	6
Cholesterol (mg)	164
Carbohydrate (g)	52
Protein (g)	9
Dietary fibre (g)	3
Sodium (mg)	963

 CHEF'S ADVICE

Allow the steamed carrot cake to set in the refrigerator overnight. This will not only ensure firmness in the final dish, but will also help the carrot cake develop its flavour.

Chwee Kueh

Chwee kueh is a steamed rice flour cake served with a savoury topping of preserved sweet radish. It was traditionally a breakfast dish, but is now sold throughout the day.

The texture and smoothness of the *chwee kueh* and the crispness of the preserved sweet radish are often used as benchmarks to identify good quality *chwee kueh*.

In the olden days, *chwee kueh* was made by milling aged rice which was believed to absorb more water to produce smooth and soft *chwee kueh*. The batter was then steamed in clay moulds to enhance the flavour of the rice flour cakes. Today, aluminium moulds and commercially milled rice flour are used.

Origins

Chwee kueh is believed to have originated in southern China, from the Hokkiens or Teochews, as a way of stretching rice supplies. *Chwee kueh* can still be found in Shantou today.

Variations

The modern version of *chwee kueh* is made with rice flour and starch (such as tapioca flour) to increase the smoothness of the rice flour cake. The topping is made by cooking preserved sweet radish with dark soya sauce, minced garlic and sugar. Today, *chwee kueh* is also commonly served with sambal *belacan* (chilli with dried shrimp paste) for added spice. Variations include the addition of toasted white sesame seeds and shallot oil to enhance the flavour.

SCIENCE CONNECTION

Preserved radish is produced by sun-drying and salting chopped Chinese white radish until the water content of the radish is reduced to about 30 per cent. The radish is then harvested and kept in a sealed jar ready for use.

Unrefined sea salt is typically used for salting the radish because it contains calcium and magnesium, which increases the crispiness of the radish by firming up the pectins in the radish. The amount of salt added is 8 to 10 per cent based on the weight of the radish. This will create osmotic pressure which accelerates water loss from the radish, assisting in the process of pickling.

Right: Alternative presentation of *chwee kueh* — *chwee kueh* sandwich with minced meat and XO sauce

Chwee Kueh

Serves 4

For topping
Dried shrimps **400 g**
Preserved sweet radish
   (*tian chye poh*), chopped **150 g**

1. Soak ingredients separately in sufficient warm water to cover. Leave for 30 minutes.
2. Drain and chop finely, then set aside.

Corn oil **150 mL**
Garlic, peeled and minced **15 g**
Shallot, peeled and minced **15 g**

3. Heat oil in a pan over medium heat and stir-fry dried shrimps until fragrant.
4. Add garlic, shallot and preserved sweet radish. Stir-fry until mixture darkens and is fragrant.

Dark soya sauce **6 g / 1 tsp**
Sugar **30 g / 2 Tbsp**
Salt **3 g / ½ tsp**
Ground white pepper **a dash**

5. Add to pan and stir-fry for another 20 minutes.

White sesame seeds,
   toasted **15 g**

6. Add to pan and mix well. Set aside and keep warm.

Rice flour **120 g**
Tapioca flour **8 g / 2 tsp**
Salt **3 g / ½ tsp**
Corn oil **20 g / 2 Tbsp**

7. Combine ingredients in a mixing bowl.

Water **330 mL**

8. Add water and whisk well.

Water, boiling **500 mL**
Corn oil **as needed**

9. Add boiling water and whisk well as batter thickens.
10. Grease *chwee kueh* moulds with oil and fill with batter.
11. Steam for 15 minutes. Unmould onto serving plates.
12. Spoon topping over *chwee kueh*.
13. Serve hot.

NUTRITION PROFILE	PER SERVING (6 pieces)
Energy (kcal)	563
Total fat (g)	37
Saturated fat (g)	5
Cholesterol (mg)	27
Carbohydrate (g)	51
Protein (g)	7
Dietary fibre (g)	2
Sodium (mg)	1006

 CHEF'S ADVICE

Cook the flour mixture, stirring it gently over low heat until slightly thickened, to ensure that the final steamed product will not have a starchy taste.

Kueh Pie Tee

Kueh pie tee makes for a beautiful and delicate hors d'oeuvres, comprising a crispy top hat-shaped shell filled with finely sliced (not shredded) yam bean (*ban kuang*) and omelette, firm bean curd and prawns.

The shells, referred to as *pie tee* by the Nonyas is made using a metal mould dipped into batter and deep-fried. The filling is sweet from the yam bean, seasoned with fermented bean paste (*tau cheo*). It is similar to the filling for *popiah* prepared by the Hokkiens in the early days.

The *pie tee* shells are filled just before serving to avoid the shells absorbing the moisture from the filling and becoming soggy. The filled shells are then topped with a spicy chilli sauce and garnished with coriander leaves.

Origins

The origins of *kueh pie tee* remains a mystery although it certainly is a Peranakan dish. Baba Ong Jin Teong wrote in an issue of *The Peranakan*, a quarterly publication of the Peranakan Association in Singapore, that *kueh pie tee* was created here during the Japanese occupation.

Some experts speculate that *kueh pie tee* was the result of British influence on Peranakan culture. They believe that *kueh pie tee* was served as a snack at teatime and so the name *pie tee* could have been derived from similar sounding English words like "patty" or "pastie".

SCIENCE CONNECTION

Soya beans are rich in protein and the soya protein molecules are relatively large. In the making of fermented bean paste (*tau cheo*), the fermentation process causes microorganisms present to produce enzymes that break down these large protein molecules into smaller peptides and finally into amino acids. When these amino acids combine with the high amounts of salt used in fermentation, a distinct umami (savoury taste) flavour is achieved.

Right: Alternative presentation of *kueh pie tee* — *pie tee* in crispy rice paper with sweet garlic-chilli sauce

Kueh Pie Tee

Makes 60 pieces

For *pie tee* shells
Water **160 mL**
Eggs, beaten **85 g**

1. Combine ingredients in a small bowl and whisk well.

Plain flour **75 g**
Rice flour **65 g**
Cornflour **10 g**
Salt **3 g / ¹/₂ tsp**

2. Combine ingredients in a mixing bowl and mix well.
3. Add egg mixture and whisk to form a smooth batter.
4. Strain batter through a fine strainer twice to remove any lumps.

Corn oil **for deep-frying**

5. Heat a pot of oil to 180°C. Immerse the *pie tee* mould in the hot oil for 3 minutes.
6. Remove mould, drain off excess oil quickly and dip into batter. Immerse mould back into hot oil.
7. Gently shake mould in a up-and-down motion, to loosen the shell from the mould. Use a bamboo skewer to release the shell if necessary. Deep-fry until golden brown.
8. Place on paper towels to drain off excess oil.
9. Repeat steps 5 to 8 until batter is used up.
10. Once shells are cool, store in an airtight container until needed.

For filling
Water **360 mL**
Salt **5 g / 1 tsp**

11. Combine in a medium pot and bring to a boil.

Pork belly **80 g**

12. Blanch in the boiling water. Remove and set aside to cool. Cut into 5-mm x 3-mm strips. Reserve the pork cooking liquid and set aside.

Corn oil **30 g / 3 Tbsp**
Firm bean curd (*tau kua*), cut into 5-mm strips **200 g**
Garlic, peeled and minced **40 g**
Fermented bean paste (*tau cheo*) **40 g**
Canned young bamboo shoots, julienned and boiled **160 g**
Yam bean (*ban kuang*), peeled and finely sliced **500 g**

13. Heat oil in a medium pot and lightly brown firm bean curd strips.
14. Add garlic and stir-fry until fragrant.
15. Add fermented bean paste and stir-fry until fragrant.
16. Add pork belly strips and stir-fry for 1 minute.
17. Add bamboo shoots and yam bean and stir-fry until yam bean is semi-tender.

Sugar **3 g / ¹/₂ tsp**
Salt **3 g / ¹/₂ tsp**

18. Add reserved pork cooking liquid to pot. Season and bring to a boil.
19. Lower heat, cover and simmer for 30 minutes, stirring occasionally.

For chilli sauce
Fresh red chillies **100 g**
Garlic, peeled **30 g**
Water **120 mL**

20. Combine ingredients in a blender and blend into a fine paste.

Rice vinegar **12 g / 1 Tbsp**
Calamansi lime juice **12 g / 1 Tbsp**
Light soya sauce **5 g / 1 tsp**
Sugar **10 g / 2 tsp**
Salt **5 g / 1 tsp**

21. Heat a saucepan over medium heat and stir-fry paste until fragrant.
22. Add ingredients to saucepan and mix until sugar dissolves. Remove from heat and set aside.

For garnishing
Medium-size prawns, peeled, deveined and halved **500 g / about 60**
Omelette, thinly sliced **200 g**
Fried shallots **100 g**
Coriander leaves **30 g / 4 sprigs**

23. Bring a pot of water to a boil and cook prawns. Drain and set aside.
24. Fill each *pie tee* shell up to three-quarters full with filling.
25. Top with a prawn, some omelette, fried shallots and coriander leaves.
26. Serve immediately with chilli sauce on the side.

NUTRITION PROFILE	PER SERVING (6 pieces)
Energy (kcal)	348
Total fat (g)	16
Saturated fat (g)	4
Cholesterol (mg)	251
Carbohydrate (g)	24
Protein (g)	28
Dietary fibre (g)	2
Sodium (mg)	648

 CHEF'S ADVICE
Assemble *pie tee* prior to eating to prevent the shells from absorbing the moisture from the filling and turning soggy.

Lor Mai Kai

Lor mai kai simply means glutinous rice with chicken in Cantonese. This classic dim sum dish is traditionally wrapped with dried lotus leaves and steamed.

The main ingredient in this dish is glutinous rice, a type of short grain rice that is sometimes also called sticky rice. When cooked, the rice grains plump up and become translucent. The texture of the cooked rice should be tender, yet firm.

The ingredients used in this dish, from the chicken to the mushrooms, sausages and rice are well marinated to yield a highly fragrant and flavourful dish.

Origins

Lor mai kai is a Cantonese dish originating from Guangdong province in China. It was brought to South East Asia by immigrants in the 19th century and became a popular food item served in teahouses and Cantonese-run restaurants in the early years.

Today, *lor mai kai* can be found packaged in disposable foil containers available for takeaway from coffee shops and dim sum shops. These handy takeaway packs are also available frozen from supermarkets.

Variations

The Chinese Dumpling Festival (*duan wu jie*) is celebrated with glutinous rice dumplings (*zongzi* in Chinese and *chang* in Hokkien) wrapped in bamboo leaf cones. In the early years, these rice dumplings had a filling similar to *lor mai kai,* but over time, variations were introduced, such as vegetarian fillings and sweet fillings.

Banh chung is the Vietnamese variant of *lor mai kai.* It is considered an auspicious dish and is typically prepared to celebrate the Lunar New Year in Vietnam. Shaped like a squarish brick, the dumpling is filled with glutinous rice, mung beans and pork, then wrapped in banana leaves and steamed. The steamed ingredients can also be deep-fried before eating.

SCIENCE CONNECTION

The stickiness of rice is dependent on its starch components. Starch is made of two types of large carbohydrate molecules called amylose and amylopectin. The amount of amylose and amylopectin varies depending on the type of grains. Long grain rice which tends to be separate, firm and fluffy after cooking contains approximately 20 per cent amylose and 80 per cent amylopectin. Glutinous rice, on the other hand, has a high amount of amylopectin and no amylose. This is why glutinous rice is very sticky when cooked.

Right: Alternative presentation of *lor mai kai* — steamed lotus leaf rice parcel with fermented soya bean-chilli sauce

Lor Mai Kai

Makes 8 portions (approximately 150 g per portion)

For chicken

Ginger, peeled and grated **10 g**
Water, hot **60 g / 4 Tbsp**

1. Combine and soak for 10 minutes. Discard ginger and retain liquid.

Chicken thigh, boneless **400 g**

2. Remove skin from chicken and cut into 2-cm cubes. Place in a big bowl.

Sesame oil **30 g / 3 Tbsp**
Hua diao jiu **30 g / 2 Tbsp**
Light soya sauce **15 g / 1 Tbsp**
Dark soya sauce **6 g / 1 tsp**
Sugar **5 g / 1 tsp**
White pepper powder **5 g / 1 tsp**
Salt **a pinch**
Water **200 mL**
Cornflour **50 g**

3. Add ingredients and ginger liquid to bowl of chicken cubes and mix well.
4. Cover and refrigerate for at least 10 hours or overnight.

For mushrooms and Chinese sausage

Dried Chinese mushrooms **15 g**
Chinese sausages **60 g**

5. Soak mushrooms in hot water for 10 minutes and drain. Cut mushroom into thick slices.
6. Soak Chinese sausages in hot water for 10 minutes and drain. Remove wax casing from Chinese sausages and slice thinly.

Water **45 g / 3 Tbsp**
Oyster sauce **15 g / 1 Tbsp**
Hua diao jiu **15 g / 1 Tbsp**
Sesame oil **3 g / 1 tsp**
Light soya sauce **3 g / ¹/₂ tsp**

7. Combine mushrooms, Chinese sausage, and remaining ingredients in a bowl and mix well.
8. Cover and set in the refrigerator for at least 10 hours or overnight.

For rice

Glutinous rice **250 g**

9. Soak in water overnight. Drain.

Water **150 mL**

10. Combine with soaked rice in a shallow container and steam for 20 minutes.

Sugar **30 g / 2 Tbsp**
Salt **1 g**
White pepper powder **1 g**
Chinese five-spice
    powder **1 g**
Sesame oil **10 g / 1 Tbsp**

11. Combine and add to steamed rice. Mix well.
12. Grease 8 small metal bowls.
13. Spoon in equal amounts of chicken and 1 Tbsp chicken marinade.
14. Add equal amounts of mushrooms and Chinese sausages.
15. Portion out rice equally into each bowl, pressing down firmly from the top.
16. Steam for 25 minutes.
17. Remove and invert onto serving plates.
18. Serve hot.

NUTRITION PROFILE	PER SERVING
Energy (kcal)	277
Total fat (g)	12
Saturated fat (g)	3
Cholesterol (mg)	50
Carbohydrate (g)	25
Protein (g)	16
Dietary fibre (g)	1
Sodium (mg)	425

 CHEF'S ADVICE
Handle the rice grains gently to keep them whole and retain their shape.

Nonya Kaya

Nonya *kaya* is a coconut egg jam, and *kaya* spread on toast is popularly eaten for breakfast as well as a snack at any time of the day in Singapore.

Origins Toast is thought to have been introduced to Singapore by the British, and *kaya* toast is said to have originated from the Hainanese who worked for British colonial officers as cooks. These Hainanese cooks are believed to have learnt to prepare toast and coffee in accordance with British culinary preferences, after which they set up their own businesses and coffee shops, and popularised toast and coffee. Some of these coffee shops still exist today.

One of these shops is Chin Mee Chin Coffee and Cake Shop at Katong. It was set up in the 1930s and still retains its original coffee shop form. Another is Killiney Kopitiam which was set up in 1919 along Killiney Road. It is the oldest coffee shop on record in Singapore. A third is Ya Kun, a Hainanese coffee shop that started in 1940s and has since expanded with outlets all over the country, many of which are franchised.

The Hainanese cooks were introduced to a wide variety of spreads for breads when they worked for the British officers, and when they started their own shops, they substituted these spreads with the local Nonya *kaya* which was made with coconut milk, eggs, pandan leaves and sugar. The characteristically thin brown toast that is served is believed to have been created out of necessity, in order to keep prices low and affordable for the masses during the early days.

It is interesting to note that this local toast was originally consumed mainly by the Eurasian community, possibly because they were more likely to have been familiar with eating Western food such as bread and toast.

Variations
Nonya *kaya* with local toast does not have many variations, except that stalls using the original ingredients are comparatively rare and considerably more expensive. The original form of the dish consisted of handmade *kaya*, which was slathered on brown bread toasted over a charcoal grill.

Today, the charcoal grill is no longer used due to health and safety concerns. Instead, electric toasters or grills are used to prepare the toast. The *kaya* in turn has become so popular that they are now mass produced and packaged in attractive jars to be sold for enjoying at home or giving away as gifts.

SCIENCE CONNECTION

Eggs are rich in protein and in the making of *kaya*, the thickening of the mixture is dependent on these protein molecules. During cooking, the heat breaks the bonds in these protein molecules and causes them to change their shape and original characteristics. This makes the eggs lose their ability to flow and instead thicken up as a result of the coagulation of the protein molecules. This leads to the thickening of the *kaya* mixture.

Egg proteins coagulate between 65°C and 70°C. However, the added sugar and coconut milk raises the coagulation temperature and continuous stirring of the mixture while heating helps to break the protein bonds during coagulation, resulting in firm *kaya* paste.

Right: Alternative presentation of Nonya *kaya* —
espuma *kaya* cream flavoured with Malibu Rum

Nonya Kaya

Makes approximately 440 g

Eggs **285 g**
Sugar **285 g**

1. Place in a heatproof mixing bowl and whisk together.

Coconut milk **200 mL**
Pandan leaves, cleaned
   and knotted **2**

2. Add coconut milk and place mixing bowl over a pot of boiling water.
3. Add pandan leaves.
4. Stir mixture continuously with a spatula for 20 minutes until mixture thickens slightly.
5. Remove pandan leaves and strain mixture into a clean mixing bowl.
6. Return to heat and stir mixture for another 10 minutes until it thickens slightly.
7. Immediately transfer to clean and dry glass containers and fill to the top. Tightly seal containers for storage.

NUTRITION PROFILE	PER SERVING (1 tsp / 20 g)
Energy (kcal)	98
Total fat (g)	4
Saturated fat (g)	3
Cholesterol (mg)	53
Carbohydrate (g)	15
Protein (g)	2
Dietary fibre (g)	<1
Sodium (mg)	22

CHEF'S ADVICE

Ensure that the mixture is maintained at 80°C during cooking and that it is stirred constantly. Going beyond 80°C will overcook the *kaya* mixture. Stirring will ensure that the *kaya* is smooth and not lumpy.

Rojak

Rojak is a salad of fresh vegetables and fruits, tossed in a sweet, sour and spicy sauce, garnished with ground peanuts. Evolving from the Indonesian salad, *rujak*, *rojak* is sold by both Chinese and Malay vendors in Singapore and is enjoyed as a snack or side dish.

The term *rojak* in local parlance means "jumbled" or "mixed up". As befitting its name, *rojak* reflects a mixture of elements from Chinese and Malay cultures.

Buah nam nam (*Cynometra cauliflora*) was included in Chinese *rojak* in the olden days, but the common ingredients used in *rojak* these days are cucumber, pineapple, yam bean (*ban kuang*), bean sprouts, freshly toasted fried bean curd puffs (*tau pok*) and dough fritters (*you tiao*). Some *rojak* stalls also add water spinach (*kangkong*), rose apple (*jambu air*), green apple, green mango, century egg, grilled dried cuttlefish and even jellyfish. Malay *rojak* may include tempeh (fermented soya bean cake).

The ingredients are cut into bite-size pieces and tossed in a dark, pungent sauce made from black shrimp paste (*haeko* or *petis udang*), chilli paste, sugar, tamarind juice, lime juice and water. Finely sliced torch ginger bud, grated lime zest and ground peanuts are then sprinkled over the salad. The finished dish is crunchy, sweet, sour and spicy.

Variations and similar dishes
The most common variation of *rojak* is fruit *rojak*, or *rojak buah campur,* which uses mainly fruits such as red and green apples, pear, Chinese pear, pineapple, guava, green mango, young papaya, and yam bean (*ban kuang*). Penang fruit *rojak* also includes starfruit and rose apple (*jambu air*) and less common fruits such as *buah kedondong* (or *buah long long*), the fruit of the ambarella tree. In Singapore, a variation of *rojak*, the white *rojak*, was introduced around 2005. This version is suitable for vegetarians and those with shrimp allergies as it uses sour plum paste instead of black shrimp paste (*haeko*).

Rojak bandung is another variation of *rojak*. It consists of boiled *kangkong*, cucumber and cuttlefish, and is dressed with a similar black shrimp paste sauce, but with added garlic and chilli paste.

Indian *rojak*, sold only by Indian vendors, is not a variation of Chinese and Malay *rojak*. Although it is called *rojak*, it is a completely different dish and uses very different ingredients and condiments.

SCIENCE CONNECTION

The torch ginger bud used in this recipe is actually the flower bud of the torch ginger plant (*Etlingera elatior*). Its flowers are widely cultivated as a spice for curry, its fruits are used to treat ear ache, and its leaves are applied to heal wounds and are also used by women who had just given birth to get rid of body odour. This flower of *E. elatior* is also known to contain several flavonoid compounds that have anti-inflammatory properties and cardioprotective effects. One such flavonoid is quercetin which is said to help reduce the risk of plaque build-up in arteries that can lead to heart attack or stroke.

Right: Alternative presentation of *rojak* —
stuffed grilled bean curd pocket with fruit and vegetable salad

Rojak

Serves 4

AROMA
Heady aroma of black shrimp paste (*haeko*) interspersed with the refreshing floral and citrus notes of the torch ginger bud

FLAVOUR PROFILE
Well-balanced savouriness of black shrimp paste and sweetness of fruits and vegetables, punctuated with sour notes of tamarind and lime juices

MOUTHFEEL
Exciting interplay of crunchy and juicy vegetables and fruits mixed with the dry and crispy dough fritters (*you tiao*)

For dressing
Tamarind pulp **20 g**
Water **15 g / 1 Tbsp**

1. Combine ingredients and mix well. Strain to obtain 20 g tamarind juice.

Sugar **30 g / 2 Tbsp**
Lime juice **12 g / 1 Tbsp**

2. In a mixing bowl, combine tamarind juice with sugar and lime juice. Mix well until sugar dissolves.

Black shrimp paste (*haeko*)
   100 mL

3. Add to mixture and mix well.

For salad
Pineapple, oblique cut **250 g**
Yam bean, oblique cut **60 g**
Cucumber, oblique cut **60 g**
Dough fritters (*you tiao*), lightly toasted and sliced (see page 166) **60 g**
Torch ginger bud, finely sliced **5 g**

4. Add to dressing.
5. Toss to coat evenly.

For garnishing
Roasted skinned peanuts, coarsely ground **60 g**

6. Sprinkle with ground peanuts and toss well.
7. Portion onto serving plates.
8. Serve at room temperature.

NUTRITION PROFILE	PER SERVING
Energy (kcal)	308
Total fat (g)	11
Saturated fat (g)	3
Cholesterol (mg)	14
Carbohydrate (g)	49
Protein (g)	7
Dietary fibre (g)	3
Sodium (mg)	679

CHEF'S ADVICE

When making the dressing, use dark brown sugar instead of white sugar for a rich caramel flavour and more attractive colour.

Roti Prata

Roti prata is a pan-fried Indian bread served with savoury or sweet accompaniments such as meat or vegetable curries and sugar. Described as "the croissant of the east", *roti prata* is traditionally sold by Indian Muslim vendors in Singapore.

Originally made with durum wheat flour (*atta*), *roti prata* is now made with refined white flour in Singapore as it produces more gluten and makes for a more elastic dough. The making of *roti prata* is often impressive, as the dough is twirled, flipped and tossed in the air. The stretched dough is then folded and cooked on a hot flat pan. This final product is a pancake that is golden brown and crisp on the exterior, yet soft and flaky inside.

Origins *Roti prata* was brought to Singapore by Indian immigrants, but the origins of the dish remains unclear. Some say it was created by the Indian Muslims from Chennai, while other believe it originated from the Punjab region where it was called *parontay* or *prontha*. And indeed, the dish goes by different names in different parts of India. In south India and Bengal, it is called *parotta* (also spelt *porotta* or *barotta*), and in north India, it is *paratha*. It is also known variously as *kothu parotta* in Sri Lanka, *roti canai* in Malaysia, *farata* in Mauritius and the Maldives, *palata* and *htat ta ya* in Myanmar, and *buss-up shot* in Trinidad and Tobago.

Variations and similar dishes *Roti prata* is a versatile dish that lends itself well to different tastes and variations. Tissue *prata* is a thin, crisp *prata* usually served in the shape of a cone. Coin *prata* is a small and thick *prata*. Modern creations include sweet and savoury fillings or toppings. Common savoury fillings include egg (plaster *prata*) and sliced onion. Innovative vendors have also come up with a variety of flavours such as chicken floss, cheese, mushroom, *keema* (minced mutton curry), chicken, seafood, sausage, potato (known as *aloo*), garlic, etc., and various combinations of such ingredients as a filling for *prata*. Sweet versions are enjoyed as dessert, with fruit fillings such as bananas, strawberries and durian, or topped with ice cream and drizzled with honey or chocolate sauce.

Murtabak is a larger, more substantial *prata* that is stuffed with minced or sliced meat, onion, garlic and eggs.

Roti prata can also be made into *kati rolls* — a burrito-like snack with grilled meat chunks and raw sliced or diced onion, cucumber and tomato.

SCIENCE CONNECTION

When making a bread like *roti prata*, it is important that the dough is sufficiently kneaded and rested to ensure a desirable final product. Sufficient kneading will help to strengthen the gluten structure and allow the dough to be stretched as thin as possible without tearing. Sufficient resting will allow the dough to be extensible so that it will not retract when stretched. The leavening of the *roti prata* dough is similar to that of baklava and strudel. The layers of dough are separated by a layer oil. When the dough is heated, the water in the dough changes to steam, expanding the space between the layers of dough. This leavens the *roti prata*, creating the flakiness.

Right: Alternative presentation of *roti prata* —
masala potato wrap with cucumber raita

Roti Prata

Makes 10 pieces (approximately 90 g per piece)

Plain flour **600 g**
Salt **10 g / 2 tsp**
Sugar **15 g / 1 Tbsp**

1. Combine dry ingredients in a mixing bowl and mix well.

Water **300 mL**
Egg, beaten **55 g / 1**
Corn oil **10 g / 1 Tbsp**

2. Add liquid ingredients and mix together. Set aside for 30 minutes.
3. Knead by hand for 10 minutes.
4. Place in a bowl and cover with a damp cloth. Set aside to rest for 30 minutes.
5. Knead by hand for 10 minutes, then divide dough into 10 portions. Roll each portion into a ball.
6. Coat dough balls with a layer of oil to prevent sticking.
7. Place dough balls on a tray, cover and place in the chiller to rest overnight.

Corn oil **as needed**

8. Oil a tabletop and flatten a ball of dough with your palm.
9. Continue to flatten and stretch the dough out on the tabletop until it is well-stretched and thin.
10. Drizzle some oil on the stretched dough. Fold the dough in from 4 sides to get a square shape.
11. Repeat steps 8 to 10 for the rest of the dough.
12. Heat some oil in a flat non-stick pan over medium heat. Fry the dough until golden brown on each side. Remove.
13. Fluff and flake the *prata* by pressing the sides of the *prata* towards its centre with your palms in a quick "clapping" motion.
14. Serve hot with fish head curry (page 72).

NUTRITION PROFILE	PER SERVING (2 pieces)
Energy (kcal)	448
Total fat (g)	9
Saturated fat (g)	1
Cholesterol (mg)	37
Carbohydrate (g)	79
Protein (g)	11
Dietary fibre (g)	2
Sodium (mg)	1100

CHEF'S ADVICE

Water can be substituted for milk to give a fuller flavour to the *roti prata* and at the same time, mask some of the doughy flavour.

Desserts

Bubor Cha Cha

Bubor is the Malay word for "porridge" and *cha cha* is the Hokkien term for "abundance". Hence, the name of this dessert translates to "porridge of abundance".

And indeed, this dessert of Malay origin is chock-full of sweet potato and yam cubes, and colourful tapioca balls, bathed in sweetened coconut milk.

Generally, *bubor cha cha* is made by dissolving sugar in boiling water and cooking the syrup with pandan leaves to extract its fragrant aroma. Coconut milk is added, followed by cubes of sweet potato and yam. The tubers are then simmered over low heat until tender. The colourful tapioca balls are cooked separately and added to the sweet dessert only upon serving. *Bubor cha cha* can be enjoyed hot or cold.

The main ingredient defining the taste of this Malay dessert is sugar. Traditionally, palm sugar was used as a sweetener, but food stalls serving this dessert typically use white sugar today.

Variations The traditional *bubor cha cha* recipe features sweet potatoes, yam, white beans and banana (specifically *pisang raja,* a local banana) in a sweetened coconut milk soup, but modern versions omit the white beans and banana, and include coloured tapioca balls and coloured sago flour cubes. Some variations may also include strips of jackfruit and slices of banana.

In Thailand, a similar dessert is served with red rubies (cubes of red-coloured water chestnuts coated with a clear starchy coating of arrowroot flour) in a sweetened coconut milk soup.

SCIENCE CONNECTION

Sweet potatoes belong to the same botanical family as the morning glory. Sweet potatoes are excellent sources of beta-carotene (a precursor of vitamin A), B vitamins, dietary fibre and minerals. They are also fat-free and relatively low in sodium. There are several varieties of sweet potatoes, including the yellow- and orange-fleshed varieties used in this recipe, and a purple-fleshed variety. Purple sweet potatoes are naturally rich in the pigment, anthocyanin, that offers its rich purple colour. Not only are these pigments heat and light stable, they are also known to be strong antioxidants that are often associated with health preventive effects and reduced risks of certain diseases, such as cardiovascular disorders and cancer. Some studies have indicated that anthocyanins are able to boost immunity and that they display anti-inflammatory properties to some extent.

Right: Alternative presentation of *bubor cha cha* —
coconut granita with sous vide osmanthus sweet potato cubes

Bubor Cha Cha

Serves 4

AROMA
Distinct aroma of coconut and pandan

FLAVOUR PROFILE
Sugary sweetness against a strong coconut cream flavour with a note of pandan

MOUTHFEEL
Warm, rich and creamy with chewy tapioca cubes and tender sweet potato and yam cubes

---

Water **60 g / 4 Tbsp**
Food colouring, red or green **5 drops**

1. Combine in a small pot and bring to a boil.

Tapioca flour **50 g + more for dusting**

2. Place in a mixing bowl and add the boiling coloured water. Mix well to form a dough.
3. Dust a tabletop with some tapioca flour.
4. Place dough on tabletop and knead until smooth.
5. Roll dough into a thin rod and cut into small pieces.
6. Roll pieces lightly to shape into balls.

Water **300 mL**
Sugar **15 g / 1 Tbsp**

7. Combine in a pot and bring to a boil.
8. Add tapioca balls and cook for 20 minutes or until the balls float.
9. Remove and soak in an ice bath until the balls turn transparent. Drain and set aside.

Yam **60 g**
Yellow sweet potatoes **60 g**
Orange sweet potatoes **60 g**
Pandan leaves, cleaned and knotted **6**

10. Peel and cut yam and sweet potatoes into 2-cm cubes.
11. Place ingredients on a steaming tray and steam for 20 minutes until tubers are tender.
12. Discard pandan leaves. Set tubers aside.

Water **350 mL**
Coconut cream **300 mL**
Pandan leaves, cleaned and knotted **12**

13. Combine ingredients in a medium pot and simmer over low heat for 25 minutes until pandan leaves darken.

Rock sugar **75 g**
Salt **a pinch**

14. Add to pot together with tubers and tapioca balls. Mix well.
15. Serve hot or chill to serve cold.

NUTRITION PROFILE	PER SERVING
Energy (kcal)	463
Total fat (g)	31
Saturated fat (g)	27
Cholesterol (mg)	0
Carbohydrate (g)	49
Protein (g)	4
Dietary fibre (g)	3
Sodium (mg)	62

 CHEF'S ADVICE

While preparing the other ingredients, keep the cut yam and sweet potatoes submerged in water to prevent discolouration.

Chendol

Chendol is a popular cold dessert found in Indonesia, Malaysia, Singapore, Thailand and Vietnam. It can be easily identified from the strips of vivid green jelly, made by mixing pandan juice with rice flour.

The jelly is added to sweetened coconut milk and topped with cooked red beans and generous amounts of palm sugar syrup.

Origins

It has been said that the name "*chendol*" originated from the Indonesian word "*jendol*", which means "bulge", a reference to the sensation experienced when the generous serving of green jelly is swallowed whole.

In an article published in *The Straits Times* in 1952, the then Governor of Singapore, Mr J.F. Nicoll, described *chendol* as a "Malayan thirst-quencher made of iced coconut milk and *gula malaka*."

And indeed, the dessert can be found throughout South East Asia, making it hard to trace the origins of *chendol* with certainty.

Variations In Singapore, *chendol* is often served with
nipa palm fruit (*attap chee*), sweet corn and grass jelly in addition
to the ubiquitous green jelly and red beans. Some versions also
incorporate kidney beans, which are larger and meatier compared to
normal red beans.

Other innovations include durian *chendol*, served with a topping
of fresh durian paste. This variation tastes radically different due to
the overpowering flavour of the durian paste.

Nonya *chendol* (also known as *tai bak*) is similar in form to
common *chendol*, but the taste is different, as the jelly is made from
a mixture of rice flour and tapioca flour, instead of mung bean flour
and cornflour.

SCIENCE CONNECTION

When the *chendol* paste comes into contact with water, a chemical
process called gelatinisation occurs, where the amylose molecules
in the paste (starch) move into the cooking water (*see also* page 164).
As the paste cools due to the cold water, these free amylose
molecules in the surrounding liquid slowly lose their energy
to flow around and come together to form a network, trapping
water as well as starch granules inside. This results in the formation
of a starch gel. Thus, it is crucial to let the *chendol* jelly sit in the iced
water for at least 15 minutes to ensure it has enough time to form a gel.
As this gel is formed with amylose, it is important to use starches
of high amylose value. The starches used here, mung bean flour
and cornflour, have amylose value of 28 per cent and 31 per cent
respectively, which are among the highest of all starches. This makes
them excellent ingredients for making *chendol*.

Right: Alternative presentation of *chendol* —
chendol gelato bar with palm sugar emulsion

Chendol

Serves 4

Ingredients	Method
Red beans **45 g** Water **80 mL**	1. Combine in a bowl and set aside to soak overnight.
Water **1 L** Rock sugar **15 g**	2. Drain red beans and place in a pot with water. Bring to a boil. 3. Simmer over medium heat for 1 hour. 4. Add rock sugar and simmer for another hour. 5. Drain and set red beans aside.
Pandan leaves, cleaned and knotted **3** Water **240 mL**	6. Combine in a blender and strain to obtain 180 mL pandan juice.
Mung bean flour **12 g / 1 Tbsp** Cornflour **12 g / 1 Tbsp** Alkaline water **3 drops**	7. Prepare a bowl of iced water and a piping bag fitted with a 0.4-cm diameter tip. Set aside. 8. In a pot, combine both types of flour, alkaline water and pandan juice. 9. Cook over medium heat, stirring continuously until mixture turns into a green translucent paste. 10. Immediately spoon paste into prepared piping bag and pipe short lengths of paste into prepared bowl of iced water. 11. Let paste sit in iced water for 15 minutes. Drain and set aside.
Coconut milk **120 mL** Salt **a pinch**	12. Combine in a small pot and bring to a boil. Set aside to cool.
Palm sugar, chopped **150 g** Water **75 mL / 5 Tbsp** Pandan leaf, cleaned and knotted **1**	13. Combine in a medium pot and stir continuously over medium heat until palm sugar has melted. 14. Simmer for 1 minute and set aside.
Shaved ice **800 g**	15. Evenly portion out red beans, jelly and palm sugar syrup into 4 bowls. Top with shaved ice and drizzle with coconut milk. Serve immediately.

NUTRITION PROFILE	PER SERVING
Energy (kcal)	268
Total fat (g)	8
Saturated fat (g)	6
Cholesterol (mg)	0
Carbohydrate (g)	48
Protein (g)	3
Dietary fibre (g)	3
Sodium (mg)	115

 CHEF'S ADVICE

Let the red beans soak in the syrup overnight before serving.

The quality of palm sugar varies from manufacturer to manufacturer, so try out a few brands to identify your preferred product. If the syrup crystallises after storing, add some water and bring to a boil to adjust the consistency.

Ondeh Ondeh

Ondeh ondeh (sometimes spelt "*onde onde*" and also called "*oneh oneh*") is a popular snack of chewy sweet potato dumplings filled with melted palm sugar and covered with freshly grated coconut.

This bite-size *kueh* (a generic Malay term for Malay and Nonya cakes and pastries) is typically sold by Chinese, Malay and Peranakan vendors in Singapore.

Known as *buah melaka* in Malaysia, *ondeh ondeh* is thought to be of Malay or Nonya origin. However, it has been suggested that these dumplings originated from the traditional Indonesian snack/dessert, *klepon* — chewy rice flour balls covered with desiccated coconut and filled with palm sugar — and was adopted by the Malays and Peranakans in the region.

Ondeh ondeh is made from a sweet potato and glutinous rice flour dough, flavoured with pandan juice. It is the pandan juice that gives *ondeh ondeh* its traditional green colour. Today, colouring is added to enhance the colour.

The dough is divided into bite-size pieces, stuffed with palm sugar, and rolled into balls before being cooked in boiling water. Once cooked, the dumplings are rolled in steamed, lightly salted grated coconut. When the soft and chewy balls are bitten into, they burst, and the sweet melted palm sugar oozes out.

Variations and similar dishes *Ondeh ondeh* is

sometimes filled with grated coconut sweetened with palm sugar. More recent variations of *ondeh ondeh* include fillings such as chocolate.

Badak berendam, a Malay *kueh* usually served during Ramadan, is similar to this type of *ondeh ondeh* with its glutinous, chewy exterior and filling of coconut and palm sugar. However, instead of being coated with grated coconut, *badak berendam* is served in coconut milk.

SCIENCE CONNECTION

Why do the balls of *ondeh ondeh* float after boiling for 3 minutes? As the *ondeh ondeh* dough is kneaded, small air bubbles are trapped in the dough. When the balls are added to the boiling water, they sink as the density is higher than that of the water. After heating in the boiling water for 3 minutes, the trapped air bubbles expand sufficiently, forming air pockets that increase the volume of the *ondeh ondeh,* an increase visible even to the naked eye! As the volume increases, the density decreases to become less than that of the water, causing the balls to float. This principle also relates to the cooking of dumplings. In an indirect way, chefs have established this relationship of food floating with their doneness.

Right: Alternative presentation of *ondeh ondeh* —
pandan glutinous truffle balls with chocolate ganache dip

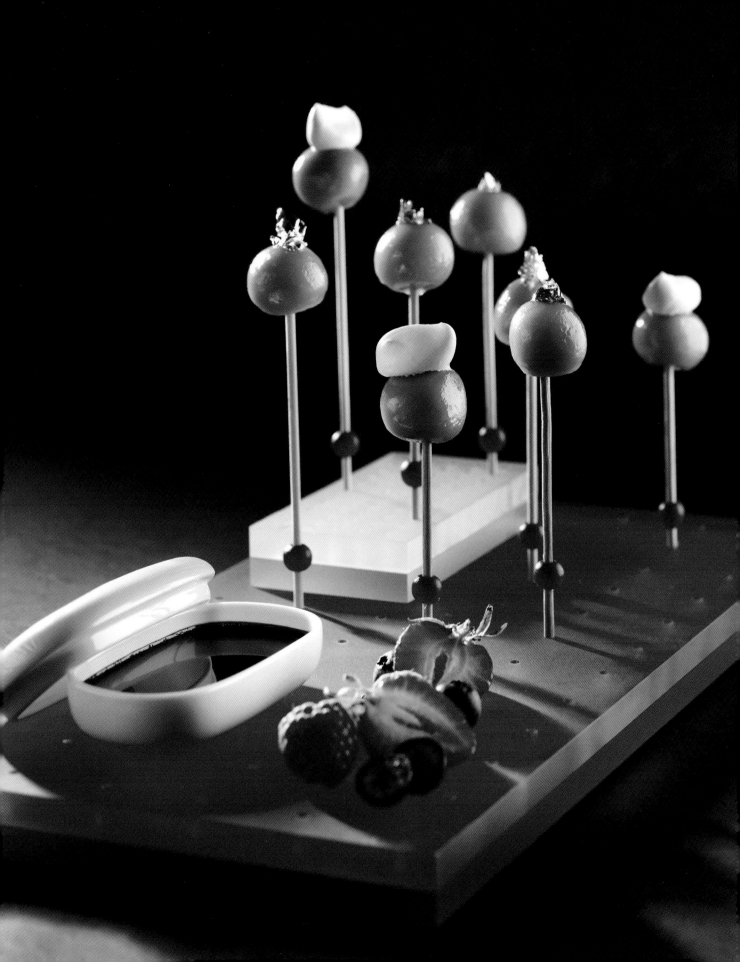

Ondeh Ondeh

Makes 9 pieces

Ingredients	Method
Sweet potato, peeled and thickly sliced **100 g**	1. Place in a steamer and steam until tender. Set aside.
Pandan leaf, cleaned and knotted **1** Water **35 mL / 2 Tbsp**	2. Combine in a blender and strain to obtain 60 g pandan juice.
Sugar **15 g / 1 Tbsp**	3. Blend with sweet potato and pandan juice into a smooth paste.
Glutinous rice flour **40 g** Tapioca flour **40 g** Green food colouring (optional)	4. Combine both types of flour with sweet potato mixture. Add colouring if desired. Knead into a smooth and pliable dough. Adjust dough texture with water or flour if needed. 5. Portion dough into 10 g pieces.
Palm sugar, grated **35 g**	6. Divide palm sugar into 4 g portions and compress each portion into a ball. 7. Flatten a ball of dough in your palm and place a portion of palm sugar in the centre. 8. Enclose dough and roll between palms to shape it. 9. Repeat steps 7 to 8 until ingredients are used up.
Freshly grated coconut **100 g** Salt **a pinch**	10. Mix well. Place in a steamer and steam for 5 minutes and set aside. 11. Bring a pot of water to a boil. 12. Lower in dough balls and boil for 3 minutes or until the balls float. 13. Drain well and coat with steamed grated coconut. 14. Serve at room temperature.

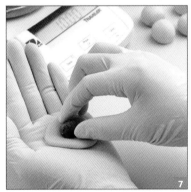

NUTRITION PROFILE	PER SERVING (3 pieces)
Energy (kcal)	250
Total fat (g)	7
Saturated fat (g)	6
Cholesterol (mg)	0
Carbohydrate (g)	46
Protein (g)	2
Dietary fibre (g)	3
Sodium (mg)	130

 CHEF'S ADVICE

The moisture content of sweet potatoes varies between varieties. Additional water may be added to the dough if it is not pliable.

Select dark green pandan leaves for better flavour. The chlorophyll will also enhance the colour of the *ondeh ondeh*.

Tau Suan with Dough Fritters

Tau suan is a sweet dessert made by steaming split yellow mung beans for long hours until tender, then mixing the softened beans with pandan-flavoured syrup.

The syrup is then thickened with potato starch or water chestnut flour, giving the final dish a texture resembling porridge. This dessert is usually paired with Chinese dough fritters, also called *you char kway* or *you tiao* meaning "fried oily sticks".

Origins
Tau suan is a Teochew dish originating from Shantou, China where it was originally prepared using whole mung beans. The Teochews were primarily farmers and mung beans were a staple.

Today, split mung beans are used to prepare this dessert in place of whole mung beans.

Variations
The original dish may not have included the slices of dough fritters which may have been added later to enhance the overall enjoyment of the dessert. In some versions of the dish, dough nuggets shaped like butterflies are added in place of the dough fritters, but they are similar in texture to the dough fritters.

SCIENCE CONNECTION

A starch slurry is made from a mixture of starch and water and used as a thickening agent in the preparation of many dishes. Heating starch in water causes the starch granules to swell up. Some starch components, mainly the amylose molecules in the starch granules, also migrate out into the cooking water. At the same time, water enters the starch granules and causes the granules to expand. This movement of amylose and water molecules causes the food to thicken or become more viscous. This process is known as gelatinisation.

Right: Alternative presentation of *tau suan* with dough fritters — vanilla mung bean jelly with caramel coconut sauce and dehydrated fritter slice

Tau Suan with Dough Fritters

Serves 6

AROMA
Delicate aroma of pandan

FLAVOUR PROFILE
Sweetness of rock sugar with slightly savoury taste of dough fritters

MOUTHFEEL
Smooth thickened syrup with tender split yellow mung beans and crispy dough fritters

For *tau suan*

Split yellow mung beans **80 g**

1. Rinse and soak overnight. Drain and repeat to rinse and drain again.
2. Place beans in a steamer and steam for 30 minutes. Set aside.

Pandan leaves, cleaned and knotted **12**
Water **750 mL**
Rock sugar **70 g**

3. Combine ingredients in a pot, cover and simmer over low heat until sugar has dissolved.

Sweet potato flour **24 g / 2 Tbsp**
Water **45 g / 3 Tbsp**

4. Combine ingredients to form a slurry.
5. Add slurry to sugar syrup and stir to thicken.
6. Gently stir in steamed mung beans. Remove pandan leaves just before serving.
7. Serve hot with dough fritters.

For dough fritters

Cake flour **500 g**
Salt **10 g / 2 tsp**
Sugar **15 g / 1 Tbsp**

8. Combine ingredients and mix well.

Ammonia bicarbonate **2 g / ¹⁄₂ tsp**
Baking soda **4 g / 1 tsp**
Water **300 mL**

9. Dissolve ammonia bicarbonate and baking soda in water. Add to the flour mixture.
10. Knead by hand to form a soft pliable dough.
11. Cover with a moist cloth and rest dough for 25 minutes.
12. Knead dough 25 times. Cover and set aside to rest for another 25 minutes.
13. Repeat to knead dough another 25 times and let it rest for 25 minutes.
14. Dust dough with flour and use a rolling pin to roll dough out into a rectangular sheet, approximately 24-cm x 26-cm x 1-cm. Cover with a damp cloth and let rest at room temperature for 4 hours.
15. Cut dough into 2-cm x 12-cm strips.
16. Brush the centre of a dough strip with water. Place another strip over it. Place a bamboo skewer on the centre of the strips and press down on it.
17. Repeat with the remaining dough strips.
18. Heat oil in a wok to 180°C. Pull both ends of a pair of dough strips until about 30-cm in length and place into hot oil.
19. Deep-fry, turning the fritter over constantly until puffed up and golden brown.
20. Remove and drain well.

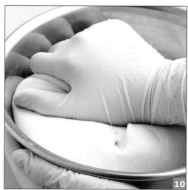

NUTRITION PROFILE	PER SERVING (Tau Suan)
Energy (kcal)	74
Total fat (g)	0
Saturated fat (g)	0
Cholesterol (mg)	0
Carbohydrate (g)	18
Protein (g)	<1
Dietary fibre (g)	1
Sodium (mg)	<1

NUTRITION PROFILE	PER SERVING (Dough Fritters, 2 pieces)
Energy (kcal)	538
Total fat (g)	28
Saturated fat (g)	4
Cholesterol (mg)	0
Carbohydrate (g)	66
Protein (g)	9
Dietary fibre (g)	2
Sodium (mg)	876

 CHEF'S ADVICE

This recipe creates a light dough fritter. For a firmer textured fritter, substitute cake flour with plain flour.

If ammonia bicarbonate is not available, replace with 5 g double-action baking powder.

GLOSSARY

Alkaline water *e.* / Air abu *m.* /
Kee chwee *h.*
Alkaline water or lye water is a solution of food-grade potassium or sodium carbonate. The alkaline water improves the texture of starchy Nonya *kuehs,* making them smooth and springy. Alkaline water is available in bottles from Asian supermarkets.

Bamboo shoots *e.* / Rebung *m.* /
Dendrocalamus asper
These young shoots of the bamboo plant are harvested just before they appear above the ground and are popularly used in South East Asian cooking. Bamboo shoots are light yellow in colour and have a soft yet crunchy texture. To prepare fresh bamboo shoots, remove the hard outer layer and boil until the shoots are tender. Canned bamboo shoots are pre-cooked and readily available from Asian supermarkets.

Bean sprouts *e.* / Tau geh *h.* /
Vigna radiata
In Singapore, bean sprouts refer to sprouts grown from mung beans. These crisp, juicy sprouts can be eaten raw or cooked and are popularly added to soups and noodle dishes.

Bird's eye chillies *e.* / Cili padi *m.* /
Capsicum annuum
Bird's eye chillies are sometimes also referred to as small red chillies or red eye chillies. Although small, these chillies are much spicier than regular red chillies and impart an extremely intense heat.

Black shrimp paste *e.* /
Petis udang *m.* / Haeko *h.*
This strong-smelling thick black paste is made from fermented shrimps, salt and sugar, and includes thickeners. It is different from dried shrimp paste (*belacan*) and should not be used as a substitute. Black shrimp paste is sold in small plastic jars. The paste can be used straight from the jar and if necessary, diluted with a small amount of warm water.

Calamansi limes *e.* / Limau kasturi *m.* /
Citrofortunella microcarpa
Also known as musk lime, these small fruits are from the citrus family. The thin-skinned fruits are only 2 to 3 cm in diameter and bear dark green skin, but when cut open, reveal rich yellow flesh. These limes are more fragrant than any other types of limes. Substitute(s): Limes, lemons, half-ripe kumquats

Candlenuts *e.* / Buah keras *m.* /
Aleurites moluccanus
With a fairly high content of oil, candlenuts provide a rich creamy, nutty flavour with a slight bitter aftertaste to dishes they are used in. The nuts are usually pounded and added to sauces and gravies to thicken them. Substitute(s): Cashew nuts

Chilli paste *e.* / Sambal *m.*
Available in bottles from supermarkets, the main ingredients in this spicy condiment are chillies and salt. Depending on the type of chilli paste, other ingredients such as dried shrimp paste (*belacan*), fish sauce, garlic, ginger and shallots may also be added to give the chilli paste secondary flavours. Chilli paste can be served on the side as a dip or added when cooking for additional heat to dishes.

Chinese celery *e.* / Saderi cina *m.* /
Kun choy *c.* / *Apium graveolensvar secalinum*
Chinese celery has long, hollow and crisp stems, and small flat leaves. It is usually added to soups and stir-fried dishes to impart aroma and flavour as a garnish.

Chinese chives *e.* / Bawang kucai *m.* /
Ku chai *h.* / *Allium tuberosum*
Also known as garlic chives, Chinese chives look similar to spring onions, but have coarser, flatter and darker green leaves. They have a stronger aroma compared to the type of chives used in Western cuisine. Chinese chives are seldom used as a garnish, but rather as an ingredient in dishes.

Chinese sausages *e.* / Lap cheong *c.*
Chinese sausages are sold in pairs, tied together with string. Typically made from pork, these air-dried sausages add a sweet flavour to dishes they are used in. Chinese sausages must be cooked before eating. They are popularly steamed, boiled or fried.

Chinese white radish *e.* / Lobak cina *m.* / Bai luo po *md.* / *Raphanus sativus*
Also called Oriental radish or daikon in Japanese, this long, white coloured root vegetable has a pungent smell and mild juicy sweet flavour. It can be eaten raw, pickled or cooked. As it can withstand long cooking without disintegrating, and it absorbs the flavours of other ingredients it is cooked with, it is popularly used in braised dishes. In Singapore, this vegetable is sometimes also referred as the white carrot.

Chye sim *h.* / Sawi Hijau *m.* / Cai xin *md.* / *Brassica chinensis* var. *parachinensis*
Also known as Chinese flowering cabbage, this green vegetable sometimes comes with delicate tiny yellow flowers in the centre. The tender stems and leaves should be lightly cooked to retain crunchiness. *Chye sim* is popularly used in stir-fries as well as soups.

Coconut cream and milk *e.*
Coconut cream and milk are widely available and can vary in consistency and flavour depending on the brand. You will need to try them out and adjust the consistency by adding water if necessary. Coconut cream is the creamy liquid extracted from the first squeeze of the grated coconut flesh with little or no water added, while coconut milk is from the second and third extractions after the cream is obtained, with the addition of water. To obtain coconut cream, put equal amounts (in grams) of the grated coconut to water and squeeze it through a cheese cloth. Freshly squeezed coconut cream/ milk spoils easily and will keep for up to 2 days in the refrigerator.

Coriander *e.* / Ketumbar *m.* / Wan sui *h.* / *Coriandrum sativum*
Also known as cilantro and Chinese parsley, coriander is a strong-smelling herb that grows extensively in many climates throughout the world. Asian cooks use every part of the plant, from the leaves, stems and seeds to the roots. In this book, fresh coriander refers to the leaves and stem. This herb does not keep for more than a couple of days refrigerated. The best way to keep coriander fresh is to stand them in a jug of cold water and cover the stems and leaves with a plastic bag. The seeds are small brown beads that are used as a spice. They are usually dry-roasted and ground lightly to release an aromatic and mildly citrus flavour. Coriander seeds are commonly used in meat stews and curries.

Cornflour *e.*
Cornflour is also known as cornstarch. It is made from endosperm portion of corn (maize grain). Cornflour is commonly used as a thickening agent in sauces and gravies.

Curry leaves *e.* / Daun kari *m.* / *Murraya koenigii*
Curry leaves come from a hardwood tree that is indigenous to India. The small, oval leaves have a pleasing aroma that hints of tangerine and anise. The leaves are used in curries and stir-fries to add fragrance.

Dark soya sauce *e.* / Kecap pekat *m.* / Jiang you *md.*
Also referred to as black soya sauce, this condiment is much darker in colour compared to light soya sauce. It is also thicker and sweeter, and carries a wheaty aroma. Some varieties of dark soya sauce have molasses added to darken the sauce further and provide more texture. Dark soya sauce is usually added to impart colour rather than saltiness to the dish.

Dough fritters *e.* / Yu tiao *md.* / You char kway *h.*
Dough fritters are a type of traditional Chinese bread. The long dough sticks are attached in the middle and deep-fried until crispy. Dough fritters can be eaten on their own as a snack or sliced and added to sweet and savoury dishes, including *tau suan*, *rojak* and *bak kut teh*.

Dried Chinese mushrooms *e.* / Cendawan cina *m.*
This is the dried version of shiitake mushrooms which must be soaked in warm water to soften before use. Dried Chinese mushrooms have a savoury fragrance and are popularly used in vegetarian cooking. Because of their robust texture, these mushrooms need a longer cooking time than other mushrooms.

Dried shrimp paste *e.* / Belacan *m.* /
Dried shrimp paste is made by fermenting heavily salted dried shrimps or krill. The fermented mixture becomes a paste that is then moulded into blocks or flat discs and sun-dried to harden. Dried shrimp paste should be dry-roasted, either wrapped in aluminium foil or banana leaf, and placed over a flame, before using. This not only helps to release its flavour, but will also allow the paste to emit its distinct pungent aroma. It is usually used to provide a unique flavouring to savoury dishes with its smoky flavour.

Dried shrimps *e.* / Hae bee *h.*
These shelled dried shrimps are favoured in Asian cooking for the strong, distinct flavour they impart to dishes. They can be used whole, chopped or ground.

Fermented bean paste *e.* / Tau cheo *h.*
Also referred to as soya bean paste or salted soya beans, this flavourful paste is widely used in East and South East Asian cooking. It is made by salting and fermenting soya beans in a process similar to making soya sauce. The soya beans are however retained in the paste for texture and flavour.

Fermented shrimp sauce *e.* / Cincalok *m.* /
This pungent sauce is made from *gerago* shrimps which originate from Malacca, Malaysia. The shrimps are mixed with rice and salt in equal proportions, then sealed in jars and left to ferment for 3 days or more. The sauce is used as a seasoning and can also be served as a condiment, mixed with ground red chillies, shallots and lime juice.

Firm bean curd *e.* / Tahu kuning *m.* / Tau kua *h.*
As its name indicates, firm bean curd has a firm texture and can retain its shape during cooking. It is suitable for frying and braising.

Fishcakes *e.*
Fishcake is made from minced fish meat, water and salt, with some manufacturers adding wheat flour to the mixture as well. The minced fish meat is pounded until the fish protein becomes springy, meaning that the more fish protein the fishcake contains, the chewier it is. Fishcakes come in various shapes but the most common are block and cylindrical. Chilled non-fried and fried fishcake is available from Asian supermarkets.

Fish sauce *e.* / Sos ikan *m.*
Fish sauce is a thin, salty, reddish-brown liquid obtained from the fermentation of fish and salt. It is used to add saltiness and a distinct flavour to many South East Asian dishes.

Five-spice powder *e.*
Five-spice powder is made from a combination of spices, including star anise, fennel, clove, cassia bark or cinnamon, and either black pepper or Sichuan pepper. It is used in Chinese cooking for flavouring meat dishes.

Flat rice noodles *e.* / Kway teow *h.*
These broad flat rice noodles are made from rice flour. They are typically about 1-cm wide and opaque white in colour. Like rice vermicelli, these noodles are available fresh or dried. Dried flat rice noodles should be soaked in room temperature water for about 30 minutes prior to using.

Fried bean curd puffs *e.* / Tau pok *h.*
Fried bean curd puffs are light and fluffy, with a chewy texture. They are popularly added to dishes with tasty gravies and soups as they soak up the liquid and hence the flavour of the dish.

Galangal *e.* / Lengkuas *m.* /
Alpinia galanga
Galangal belongs to the same family as ginger and is also known as blue ginger. It is a large rhizome which is pale pink in colour when young and beige in colour when older. Galangal cannot be used as a replacement for ginger since its flavour and pungency are distinctively different.

Hua diao jiu *md.*
Also known as Shaoxing wine or yellow wine (*huang jiu*), this Chinese cooking wine is made from glutinous rice and wheat, water and wine starters. Traditionally, *hua diao jiu* was aged in pots decorated with floral carvings, hence its name. *Hua diao jiu* is a non-distilled wine with an alcohol level of 15 to 20 per cent.
Substitute(s): Sherry

Kaffir lime leaves *e.* /
Daun limau purut *m.* / *Citrus hystrix*
The leaves of the kaffir lime are very distinctive. They are thick and glossy, and look like two leaves joined end to end. Kaffir lime leaves add a citrusy flavour to dishes. They can be used whole or roughly torn and added to curries when cooking or finely shredded and sprinkled over salads or cooked dishes as garnish.

Laksa leaves *e.* / Daun kesom *m.* /
Persicaria odorata
Although sometimes also called Vietnamese mint, the fragrant laksa leaf is not a mint, but a close relative to basil. To use, strip the leaves from the central stem and add whole or finely sliced.
Substitute(s): Equal parts of mint and coriander leaves or Asian pennywort

Lemongrass *e.* / Serai *m.* /
Cymbopogon citratus
Widely used in South East Asian cooking, lemongrass imparts a unique fragrance and flavour that is both lemony and sweet when the stem is bruised or chopped up. It is used in savoury dishes such as curries and gravies, as well as sweet desserts. Choose young stems for the strongest flavour.

Light soya sauce *e.* / Kecap cair *m.* /
Tau yu *h.*
Sometimes simply called soya sauce, this clear, golden brown sauce is salty with a yeasty aroma due to the fermentation process of the soya beans. It is typically used in place of salt to add saltiness and flavour.

Mung bean flour *e.*
Also known as green bean flour, this fine grain starch is extracted from mung beans. It is gluten-free and can be used to make noodles and pastries because of its high protein content. Mung bean flour is also high in calcium, magnesium and phosphorous.

Okra *e.* / *Abelmoschus esculentus*
Also known as ladies' finger due to its long, slender shape, okra belongs to the hibiscus family. Used as a vegetable, okra is actually the immature fresh green pod of the okra plant. It is often cooked in stews or stir-fried.

Palm sugar *e.* / Gula melaka *m.*
Originally made from the sugary sap of the date tree, palm sugar is now made from the sap of coconut trees. The sap is boiled for 4 to 5 hours until the liquid thickens and the colour changes to golden brown. The thickened syrup is then poured into bamboo tubes and left to solidify into cylinder-shaped blocks.
Substitute(s): Brown or muscovado sugar

Pandan leaves *e.* / Daun pandan *m.* / *Pandanus amaryllifolius*
Also called screw pine leaves, pandan leaves are used in both savoury and sweet Asian dishes to provide a sweet grassy aroma and natural green colour to food. They are as essential in Asian cooking as vanilla is in Western cooking. The aroma of the leaves is released when bruised. As such, pandan leaves are normally tied into a knot, bruising the leaves, before they are added to the pot to simmer in coconut milk or sugar syrup.

Preserved radish *e.* / Lobak masin *m.* / Chai poh *h.*
Preserved radish is available in different forms, whole, thinly sliced, shredded, or finely chopped, and in two varieties, sweet or salted. Depending on the amount of salt added in the production process, the preserved salted radish may need to be soaked and rinsed before use to get rid of the excess salt.

Rice flour *e.*
Rice flour is finely milled rice and has a texture similar to that of cornflour. Rice flour is gluten-free and is often used to make certain sticky Asian cakes and sweets.

Rice vermicelli *e.* / Bee hoon *h.* / Mi fen *md.*
Rice vermicelli is made from rice flour and it is available in both fresh and dried forms and with fine or coarse strands. Dried rice vermicelli should be soaked in warm water to soften prior to using. Fresh noodles are ready to use and need not be pre-cooked.

Rock sugar *e.* / Bing tang *md.*
Considered as Chinese rock sugar, these irregularly shaped pieces of crystallised, refined sugar are not as sweet as granulated sugar and the colour varies depending on the refining process, with the clearer, whiter ones being more refined. Because of its clear taste, rock sugar is popularly used in Chinese cooking, including soups, desserts and teas.

Sweet dark soya sauce *e.* / Kecap manis *m.*
This sweet dark soya sauce is made from fermented soya beans and wheat, sweetened with palm sugar and flavoured with herbs and spices including shallots, star anise, galangal, Indonesian bay leaves (*salam* leaves), lemongrass and kaffir lime leaves.

Sweet potato flour *e.*
Sweet potato flour is dull white in colour and stiff in texture. It is high in fibre and contains a higher level of carbohydrates and lower level of proteins than common wheat flour. It can be used as a thickener for sauces and gravies, and is commonly used in gluten-free cooking and baking.

Sweet potatoes *e.* / Ubi keledek *m.* / *Ipomoea batatas*
Sweet potatoes come in various colours. This edible tuberous root is long with tapered ends. The flesh is sweet, moist and crumbly when cooked. Sweet potatoes with deeper coloured flesh are sweeter and more moist than light coloured ones.

Tamarind *e.* / Asam Jawa *m.* /
Tamarindus indica
Tamarind pulp is obtained from the ripe pods of the *tamarindus indica*. The pulp is dark brown in colour, with shiny brown seeds. Some supermarkets may stock tamarind pulp in packets, without the pods and seeds. To use, soak the pulp in warm water, kneading it to release the flavour into the water, then strain to obtain the tamarind juice. Tamarind adds a sharp sour note with a hint of sweetness to dishes it is used in.

Tapioca flour *e.*
Tapioca flour is made from starch extracted from cassava roots and is used to bind gluten-free recipes and improve the texture and crispiness of baked goods. It makes a great thickener for sauces and can be used as a substitute for cornflour.

Thick dark soya sauce
This is a thick and sweet dark soya sauce that is drizzled over chicken rice for extra flavour before eating. If thick dark soya sauce is not available in your local supermarket, make your own by mixing together equal parts of molasses (treacle), light soya sauce and brown sugar. Boil the mixture down until it is thick.

Torch ginger bud *e.* / Bunga kantan *m.* /
Etlingera elatior
Known by various other names such as ginger flower, red ginger lily, torch lily and wild ginger, the torch ginger bud is native to South East Asia and belongs to the same family as ginger. It has a delicate sweet aroma, and can be sliced and eaten raw in salads, or cooked in dishes.

Turmeric *e.* / Kunyit *m.* / *Curcuma longa*
A rhizome that is part of the ginger family, turmeric is a bright orange root, used in small quantities as a spice and food colouring. In Asian cooking, it is used in both savoury and sweet dishes.

"Yam" *e.*
In Singapore, the name "yam" is used to refer to the root vegetable, taro (*Colocasia esculenta*). It is a tuber grown in tropical areas and is widely used in cooking throughout South East Asia. It has a round, barrel-like shape with dark brown skin. The flesh is white with purple specks. Wear gloves when peeling taro as there are toxins just below the skin which can irritate your hands. The toxins are eliminated when cooked.

Yam bean *e.* / Ubi sengkuang *m.* /
Ban kuang *h.* / *Pachyrrhizus erosus*
Although it is commonly called a turnip in Singapore, this single swollen root tuber is in fact a yam bean. Containing about 10 per cent starch, this watery root tuber can be eaten raw in salads or grated and braised in stock with other vegetables as a dish.

Yellow Hokkien noodles *e.*
These yellow-coloured noodles are made by adding alkaline salts or lye water to wheat flour to provide a firm and elastic texture to the noodles. The alkaline salts or lye water give the noodles its characteristic yellow colour.

---

e. = English, m. = Malay, h. = Hokkien, md. = Mandarin

REFERENCES

Noodles and Rice

Beef Kway Teow

Chan, Margaret. "Beef noodles with a Hainanese kick." *The Straits Times,* 29 Apr 1984: 4. *NewspaperSG.* 1 Nov 2014. Web.

Chan, Margaret. "Tripe and true story of a family legacy." *The Straits Times,* 14 Jul 1988: 4. *NewspaperSG.* 1 Nov 2014. Web.

Chan, Margaret. "Canny copies with a twist." *The Straits Times,* 2 Aug 1992: SUNPLUS7. *Newslink.* 1 Nov 2014. Web.

Chopra, H.K., and P.S. Panesar. *Food Chemistry.* Oxford : Alpha Science International Ltd., 2010. Print.

Durai, Jennani. "Hidden Bangkok." *The Straits Times,* 21 Apr 2013: 11. *LexisNexis Academic.* 1 Nov 2014. Web.

Ebrahim, Naleeza. *Not Just a Good Food Guide: Singapore.* Singapore: Marshall Cavendish Editions, 2006. Print.

Fahey, Michael. "Oodles of beef noodles." *South China Morning Post:* 17. *LexiNexis Academic.* 1 Nov 2014. Web.

Ho, Michelle. "What's your beef?" *The Straits Times,* 24 Apr 2002: 8-9. *Newslink.* 1 Nov 2014. Web.

"Hock Lam Street Beef Kway Teow." *The Straits Times,* 7 Feb 2010: 7. *Newslink.* 1 Nov 2014. Web.

Makansutra Singapore 2007: The Frank & No Frills Guide to Street Food & Restaurants in Singapore. Singapore: Makansutra S. Pte, Ltd, 2006. Print.

"Make It Yourself Beef Kway Teow Soup." *The Straits Times:* 22. *Newslink.* 1 Nov 2014. Web.

McWilliams, Margaret. *Foods: Experimental Perspectives.* 7th ed. New Jersey: Pearson Prentice Hall, 2012. Print.

Tan, Christopher, and Van, Amy. *Chinese Heritage Cooking.* Singapore: Marshall Cavendish Cuisine, 2012. Print.

Tan, Dylan, et. al. "Here's the beef." *The Business Times,* 29 Sep 2012: L6-L8. *Newslink.* 1 Nov 2014. Web.

Tan, Sylvia. *Singapore Heritage Food: Yesterday's Recipes for Today's Cook.* Singapore: Landmark Books, 2004. Print.

Teo, Pau Lin. "Hakka beef balls bounce back." *The Straits Times,* 9 Oct 2005: L27. *Newslink.* 1 Nov 2014. Web.

Char Kway Teow

Berlitz, H.D., W. Grosch, and P. Schieberle. *Food Chemistry.* 4th ed. Heidelberg, Germany: Springer, 2009. Print.

"One of the hawker greats." *The New Paper,* 20 Oct 1994: 9. 27 Oct 2014. Web.

"Singapore's best char kway teow, is he the Kway Teow King?" *The New Paper,* 17 Feb 1999: 16-17. 27 Oct 2014. Web.

Tay, Leslie. *The End of Char Kway Teow and Other Hawker Mysteries.* Singapore: Epigram Books. 2010. Print.

"What is chao guo tiao? Pinyin for char kway teow." *The Straits Times,* 25 Jun 1980: 10. 27 Oct 2014. Web.

Fried Hokkien Mee

Asenstorfer, R.E., Y. Wang, and D.J. Mares. "Chemical Structure of Flavonoid Compounds in Wheat (Triticum aestivum L.) Flour that Contribute to the Yellow Colour of Asian Alkaline Noodles." *Journal of Cereal Science* 43. 1 (2006): 108–119. *Science Direct.* 25 Jan 2015. Web.

Gabriel, Vincent. Special Project Interview. 24 Feb 2005.

Hung, P.H., and D.W. Hatcher. "Ultra-performance liquid chromatography (UPLC) quantification of carotenoids in durum wheat: Influence of genotype and environment in relation to the colour of yellow alkaline noodles (YAN)." *Food Chemistry* 125. 4 (2011): 1510–1516. *Science Direct.* 25 Jan 2015. Web.

Hutton, Wendy. *Green Mangoes and Lemon Grass: Southeast Asia's Best Recipes from Bangkok to Bali.* Periplus, 2003. Print.

Karim, Roselina, and Muhammad Tauseef Sultan. *Yellow Alkaline Noodles: Processing Technology and Quality Improvement.* New York : Springer, 2014. Google Books. 20 Jan 2015. Web.

Margaret Chan. "Dish that has its roots in Singapore". *The Straits Times,* 9 Sep 1984.

Tan, Bonny. "Fried Hokkien prawn noodles." *Singapore Infopedia.* 2011. 22 Sep 2014. Web.

Hainanese Chicken Rice

Berlitz, H.D., W. Grosch, and P. Schieberle. *Food Chemistry.* 4th ed. Heidelberg, Germany: Springer, 2009. Print.

Chopra, H.K., and P.S. Panesar. *Food Chemistry.* Oxford : Alpha Science International Ltd., 2010. Print.

Tan, Christopher, and Van, Amy. *Chinese Heritage Cooking.* Singapore: Marshall Cavendish Cuisine, 2012. Print.

Tay, Leslie. *Only the Best.* Singapore: Epigram Books, 2012. Print.

Vandenberghe, Tom, and Luk Thys. *Singapore and Penang Street Food.* Singapore: Lannoo, 2013. Print.

Indian Mee Goreng

Chan, Margaret. "Punggol: Gone but fare is not forgotten." *The Straits Times,* 20 Nov 1994: SUNPLUS22. *Newslink.* Web.

Chua, Beng Huat, and Rajah, Ananda. "Hybridity, Ethnicity and Food in Singapore." Working paper no. 133. Singapore: Department of Sociology, National University of Singapore, 1997(?). Print.

Ebrahim, Naleeza, and Yaw, Yan Yee. *Not Just a Good Food Guide: Singapore. Singapore:* Marshall Cavendish Editions, 2006. Print.

Eu, Geoffrey. "Happy together." *The Business Times,* 2 Feb 2013: L10-L12. *Newslink.* Web.

Makansutra Singapore 2007: The Frank & No Frills Guide to Street Food & Restaurants in Singapore. Singapore: Makansutra S. Pte. Ltd, 2006. Print.

National Heritage Board (Singapore). *Singapore: The Encyclopedia.* Singapore: Editions Didier Millet, 2006. Print.

Tan, Bonny. "Mee goreng." *Singapore Infopedia.* National Library Board Singapore, 2010. 1 Oct 2014. Web.

Teo, Pau Lin. "Meet the legends." *The Straits Times,* 31 Jul 2005: L26-L27. *Newslink.* Web.

Wong, Edmon, Cecil Johnson and Leon Nixon. "The contribution of 4-methyloctanoic (hircinoic) acid to mutton and goat meat flavour." *New Zealand Journal of Agricultural Research, 18.3 (1975): 261-266.* Print.

Laksa

Guiguet Leal, Diego Averaldo, Mirna Aparecida Pereira, Regina Maura Bueno Franco, Nilson Branco, and Romeu Cantusio Neto. "First Report of Cryptosporidium spp. Oocysts in Oysters (Crassostrea Rhizophorae) and Cockles (Tivela Mactroides) in Brazil." *Journal of Water and Health*, 6. 4 (2008) : 527-532. *IWA Publishing Online Journals*. 16 Jan 2015. Web.

"How to tell one laksa from another?" *The New Straits Times*, 3 Oct 1999: 7. Print.

Hutton, Wendy. *Singapore Food*. Singapore: Marshall Cavendish Cuisine, 2008. Print.

Miliotis, Marianne D., and Jeffrey W. Bier. *International Handbook of Foodborne Pathogens*. New York : Marcel Dekker, 2003. Google Books. 16 Jan 2015. Web.

Senachai, P., C. Chomvarin, W. Wongboot, W. Boonyanugomol, and W. Tangkanakul. "Duplex PCR for Detection of Salmonella and Shigella spp in Cockle Samples." *The Southeast Asian Journal of Tropical Medicine and Public Health*, 44. 5 (2013) : 866-874. National Institute of Health. 18 Jan 2015. Web.

Tan, Cecilia. *Penang Nyonya Cooking*. Singapore: Times Books International, 1983. Print.

Tan, Sylvia. *Modern Nonya*. Singapore: Marshall Cavendish Cuisine, 2011. Print.

"That's not the laksa you are eating; that's Penang laksa" *The Straits Times*, 29 Jan 1999: L7. Print.

"The answer is in the noodles" *The Straits Times*, 5 Feb 1999: L10. Print.

Mee Rebus

Başan, Ghillie, and Tan, Terry. *Classic Recipes, Tastes & Traditions of Malaysia & Singapore: Sensational Dishes from Two Exotic Cuisines, with 150 Authentic Recipes Shown Step by Step in 600 Beautiful Photographs*. London: Lorenz Books, 2009. Print.

Chan, Margaret. "Streetwise Dining." *The Straits Times*, 23 Sep 1990: SUNPLUS11. *Newslink*. 25 Sep 2014. Web.

Cheong, Sam. "Slurp it all up!" *The New Straits Times*, 30 Sep 2006: 49. *LexisNexis Academic*. 25 Sep 2014. Web.

Chua, Beng Huat, and Rajah, Ananda. "Hybridity, Ethnicity and Food in Singapore." Working paper no. 133. Singapore: Department of Sociology, National University of Singapore, 1997(?). Print.

Daud, Mohammed. "Rebus." *Kamus Pelajar Lengkap: Bahasa Malaysia-Inggeris-Bahasa Malaysia*. 1992. Print.

Grabowskia, J.A., V.D. Truonga, and C.R. Daubertb. "Nutritional and Rheological Characterization of Spray Dried Sweet Potato Powder." *Food Science and Technology* 41 (2008): *206-216*. Print.

Huang, Lijie. "No Meat Mee." *The Straits Times* 2 Aug 2009: 22. *Newslink*. 25 Sep 2014. Web.

IndonesiaKaya. "Mie Celor." Online video clip. 19 Jun 2012, YouTube. 28 Sep 2014. Web.

Lee, Jack T. "Grago: A Dictionary of Singlish and Singapore English." 5 Aug 2014. 25 Sep 2014. Web.

Loh, Peggy. "A taste of Johor's famous 'mee rebus'." *The New Straits Times*, 4 Jun 2004: 7. LexisNexis Academic. 25 Sep 2014. Web.

Lum, Magdalene. "Moses' Travel Commands." *The Straits Times*, 23 Sep 2003: L6. *Newslink*. 25 Sep 2014. Web.

Mah, Kan Keng. "Grubby décor, but the grub is great." *The Straits Times*, 30 Jun 1996: SUNPLUS5. *Newslink*. 25 Sep 2014. Web.

Said, Nabilah. "Heritage at Your Doorstep." *The Straits Times*, 26 Sep 2014: C2-C3. *Newslink*. 28 Sep 2014. Web.

"Surprises in origin of some local dishes." *The Straits Times*, 5 Jan 1989: 15. *NewspaperSG*. 25 Sep 2014. Web.

Teo, Pau Lin. "Satay Sticks." *The Straits Times*. 25 Apr 2004: L32. *Newslink*. 25 Sep 2014. Web.

Zahara, Rita. *Malay Heritage Cooking*. Singapore: Marshall Cavendish Cuisine, 2012. Print.

Zainol, Vivi. "A Slurp Down Memory Lane." *The Straits Times*, 16 Jul 2004: H8. *Newslink*. 25 Sep 2014. Web.

Mee Siam

Lee, Chin Koon. *The New Mrs Lee's Cookbook: Nonya Cuisine*. Singapore: Singapore Times Editions, 2003. Print.

Lee, Geok Boi. *Classic Asian Noodles*. Singapore: Marshall Cavendish Cuisine, 2007. Print.

Hou, Gary G., ed. *Asian Noodles: Science, Technology, and Processing*. Hoboken, N.J: Wiley, 2010. Print.

Hutton, Wendy. *Singapore Food*. Singapore: Marshall Cavendish Cuisine, 2008. Print.

Ranawana, D. V., C. J. K. Henry, H. J. Lightowler and D. Wang. "Glycaemic Index of some Commercially Available Rice and Rice Products in Great Britain." *International Journal of Food Sciences and Nutrition 60 (S4)* (2009): 99-110. Print.

Tan, Sylvia. *Singapore Heritage Food: Yesterday's Recipes for Today's Cook*. Singapore: Landmark Books, 2004. Print.

Meat and Seafood

Chilli Crab

"40 good years dishing up chilli crab." *The Sunday Times, Sunday Plus*. 23 Jun 1996 Print.

"Claws and found", *The Sunday Times*, 14 Mar 2004. L21. Print.

Leong, Yee Soo. *The Best of Singapore's Recipes: Everyday Favourites*. Singapore: Times Edition, 2004. Print.

Tan, Sylvia. *Singapore Heritage Food: Yesterday's Recipes for Today's Cook*. Singapore: Landmark Books, 2004. Print.

Tan, Cecilia. *Penang Nyonya Cooking*. Singapore: Times Books International, 1983. Print.

Tan, Christopher, and Van, Amy. *Chinese Heritage Cooking*. Singapore: Marshall Cavendish Cuisine, 2012. Print.

Velisek, Jan. *The Chemistry of Food*. West Sussex, UK : Wiley Blackwell, 2014. Print.

Fish Head Curry

Mowe, Rosalind. *Southeast Asian Specialties: A Culinary Journey through Singapore, Malaysia and Indonesia*. Culinaria: Konemann, 1999. Print.

Renuka M. & Rakunathan Narayanan. "Fish head curry." *Singapore Infopedia*. 2002. 22 Sep 2014. Web.

"Singapore Fish Head Curry ... Is This Our National Dish?" *Singapore Monitor*, 5 Jan 1983: 14-15. 22 Sep 2014. Web.

Woolfe, M. L., Chaplin, M. F., & Otchere, G. (1977) Studies on the mucilages extracted from okra fruits (*Hibiscus esculentus* L.) and baobab leaves (*Adansonia digitata* L.) Journal of the Science of Food and Agriculture, 28(6): 519-529. Print.

Orh Luak

Jane, Jay-lin. "Structural features of starch granules II." *Starch: Chemistry and Technology*, 3rd Edition (pp 193-236). Ed. James N. BeMiller and Roy L. Whistler. Massachusetts: Academic Press, 2009. 193-236. Print.

McWilliams, Margaret. *Foods: Experimental perspectives, 7th edition.* New Jersey: Pearson Education, 2012. Print.

Tay, Leslie. *Only the Best.* Singapore: Epigram Books, 2012. Print.

Tay, Leslie. "Oyster Omelette got two types". 12 Nov 2009. ‹http://ieatishootipost.sg/tong-siew-oyster-omelette-got-two-types/› 12 Nov 2014. Web.

Otak Otak

Berlitz, H.D., W. Grosch, and P. Schieberle. *Food Chemistry.* 4th ed. Heidelberg, Germany: Springer, 2009. Print.

Chopra, H.K., and P.S. Panesar. *Food Chemistry.* Oxford : Alpha Science International Ltd., 2010. Print.

Nasution, Peppy. *Otak-Otak Bakar Recipe (Indonesian Grilled Fish Cake).* Indonesia Eats. 4 Sep 2014. Web.

Proudlove, R.K. *The Science and Technology of Foods.* 5th ed. Hampshire : Forbes Publications, 2009. Print.

Schonhardt, Sara. *40 of Indonesia's best dishes.* 15 Aug 2011. CNN Travel. 4 Sep 2014. Web.

Tan, Christopher, and Van, Amy. *Chinese Heritage Cooking.* Singapore: Marshall Cavendish Cuisine, 2012. Print.

Tan, Terry. *Nonya Cooking, The Easy Way.* Singapore: Times Books International, 1996. Print.

"Love grilled food?" *The Straits Times,* 19 Apr 1997: H22. Print.

Satay with Peanut Sauce

Chiam, Camilla. "Exotic satay... on in-line skates." *The Straits Times,* 4 Jun 2003: H1. *Newslink.* 17 Nov 2014. Web.

Cloake, Felicity. "How to cook the perfect chicken satay." *The Guardian,* 30 Jan 2014. *The Guardian Online.* 17 Nov 2014. Web.

Khoo, Hedy. "Daging satay goreng." *The New Paper,* 19 Aug 2012: 25. *Newslink.* 17 Nov 2014. Web.

Makansutra Singapore 2007: The Frank & No Frills Guide to Street Food & Restaurants in Singapore. Singapore: Makansutra S. Pte, Ltd, 2006. Print.

Sapawi, Tuminah. "Satay-man and kampung life at the museum." *The Straits Times,* 15 Feb 1996: L3. *Newslink.* 17 Nov 2014. Web.

Tan, Hsueh Yun. "Turkey satay." *The Straits Times,* 5 Dec 2008: 21. *Newslink.* 17 Nov 2014. Web.

Tan, Monica. "Best satay in town Satay, ole!." *The New Paper,* 10 Mar 1999: 10-11. *Newslink.* 17 Nov 2014. Web.

Tan, Sylvia. *Singapore Heritage Food: Yesterday's Recipes for Today's Cook.* Singapore: Landmark Books, 2004. Print.

Tee, Hun Ching. "Like satay? Join the club..." *The Straits Times,* 22 Jul 2001: P8. *Newslink.* 17 Nov 2014. Web.

"Where does satay come from?" *The New Paper,* 24 Nov 2013: 27. *Newslink.* 17 Nov 2014. Web.

Sharma, Ajay, Vivek Bajpai, and Kwang-Hyun Baek. "Determination of Antibacterial Mode of Action of *Allium Sativum* Essential Oil against Foodborne Pathogens using Membrane Permeability and Surface Characteristic Parameters." *Journal of Food Safety* 33 (2013): 197–208. Print.

Teochew Bak Kut Teh

McWilliams, Margaret. *Foods: Experimental Perspectives.* 7th ed. New Jersey: Pearson Prentice Hall, 2012. Print.

Mowe, R. (2007). *Southeast Asian specialties: a culinary journey through Singapore, Malaysia and Indonesia.* Singapore: Page One Publishing Private Limited.

Tay, Leslie. *The End of Char Kway Teow and Other Hawker Mysteries.* Singapore: Epigram Books. 2010. Print.

Ubbink, Job. "Turning Waste into Wealth on Bones, Stocks, and Sauce Reductions." *The kitchen as laboratory: reflections on the science of food and cooking.* Ed. Cesar Vega, Job Ubbink, and Erik Van der Linden. New York: Columbia University Press, 2013. 206-216. Print.

Light Meals and Snacks

Black Carrot Cake

"Carrot cake fried to perfection." *The Straits Times,* 30 Jul 1995: 8. Print.

"How carrot cake has evolved." *The Straits Times,* 23 Sep 1984: 7. Print.

Ippoushi, Katsunari, Hiroshi Ueda, and Atsuko Takeuchi. "Milk Prevents the Degradation of Daikon (*Raphanus Sativus* L.) Isothiocyanate and Enhances its Absorption in Rats." *Food Chemistry* 161 (2014): 176-180. Print.

Pung, Kim Ying. *Famous Street Food of Penang: A Guide and Cookbook.* Malaysia: Star Publications, 2006. Print.

Wan, Ruth and Hiew, Roger. *There's No Carrot in Carrot Cake.* Singapore: Epigram Books, 2010. Print.

Chwee Kueh

"Chwee Kueh." *The New Paper,* 26 Nov 2013. 22 Sep 2014. Web.

"Dish of the week." *The Straits Times.* 2 Jan 1983. 22 Sep 2014. Web.

Wee, Eng Hwa. *Cooking for the President: Reflections and Recipies of Mrs Wee Kim Wee.* Singapore: Epigram Books. 2010. Print.

Ellinger, R. H. Phosphates in food processing. In Thomas, E. F. (Ed.) CRC *Handbook of Food Additives, Second Edition, Volume 1* (pp. 617-765). Boca Raton, FL: CRC Press. 1973. Print.

Kueh Pie Tee

Berlitz, H.D., W. Grosch, and P. Schieberle. *Food Chemistry.* 4th ed. Heidelberg, Germany: Springer, 2009. Print.

Tan, Sylvia. *Modern Nonya.* Singapore: Marshall Cavendish Cuisine, 2011. Print.

Tay, Leslie. "Violet Oon's Kitchen: Just what is this Kueh Pie Tee?" 23 Jul 2007. ‹http://ieatishootipost.sg/violet-oons-kitchen-just-what-is-this-kueh-pie-tee/›. 29 Sep 2014. Web.

Yang, Hye Jeong, Sunmin Park, Valeriy Pak, Kyung Rhan Chung, and Dae Young Kwon. "Fermented Soybean Products and Their Bioactive Compounds." *Soybean and Health.* Ed. H. El-Shemy. INTECH Open Access Publisher, 2011. 20 Jan. 2015. Print.

Lor Mai Kai

Kime, Tom. *Asian Bites: A Feast of Flavours from Turkey through India to Japan.* London: Dorling Kindersley, 2008. Print.

Kong, Foong Ling. *The Asian Kitchen.* Singapore: Periplus Editions, 2007. Print.

McWilliams, Margaret. *Foods: Experimental Perspectives.* 7th ed. New Jersey: Pearson Prentice Hall, 2012. Print.

Simonds, Nina, Hsiung Deh-Ta. *The Food of China.* St Leonards, N.S.W.: Murdoch Books, 2001. Print.

Tan, Cecilia. *Penang Nyonya Cooking.* Singapore: Times Books International, 1983. Print.

Nonya Kaya (Coconut Egg Jam)

Chua, Alvin. "Ya Kun." *Singapore Infopedia.* 2010. 18 Nov 2014. Web.

Gaman, P.M., and K.B. Sherrington. *The Science of Food.* 4th ed. Oxford: Elsevier, 1996. Print.

McWilliams, Margaret. *Foods: Experimental Perspectives.* 7th ed. New Jersey: Pearson Prentice Hall, 2012. Print.

Naidu Ratnala Thulaja. "Chin Mee Chin Confectionary." *Singapore Infopedia.* 2003. 18 Nov 2014. Web.

Tan, Florence. *Secrets of Nyonya Cooking.* Singapore: Times Editions, 2001. Print.

Rojak

Başan, Ghillie and Tan, Terry. *A Taste of Singapore.* London: Southwater, 2011. Print.

Chan, E. W. C., Y. Y. Lim, S. K. Ling, S. P. Tan, K. K. Lim, and M. G. H. Khoo. "Caffeoylquinic Acids from Leaves of Etlingera Species." *Food Science and Technology* 42 (2009):1026–1030. Print.

Chang, Yong Qing, Swee Ngin Tan, Jean W. H. Yong, and Liya Ge. "Determination of Flavonoids in *Costus speciosus* and *Etlingera elatior* by Liquid Chromatography-Mass Spectrometry." *Analytical Letters* 45 (2012): 345–355. Print.

Lee, Geok Boi. "The fruit of the platter." *The Straits Times,* 10 Sep 1989: SUNPLUS6. *Newslink.* 17 Nov 2014. Web.

Loh, Nancy. "Living like nomads in their own home." *The Straits Times,* 2 Mar 1996: L14-L15. *Newslink.* 17 Nov 2014. Web.

Lua, Jia Min. "White rojak rocks." *The Straits Times,* 27 Mar 2011: 24. *Newslink.* 17 Nov 2014. Web.

Quek, Swee Peng. "Never mind the dhal." *The Business Times,* 22 Feb 1992. *Newslink.* 17 Nov 2014. Web.

Tan, Judith. "No-sugar rojak." *The Straits Times,* 17 Nov 2004: 14. *Newslink.* 17 Nov 2014. Web.

Tan, Rebecca Lynne. "Tangy rojak bliss." *The Straits Times,* 10 Mar 2013: 29. *Newslink.* 17 Nov 2014. Web.

Tully, Joyceline. "Street sensations." *The Business Times,* 2 Oct 2010: L4-L5. *Newslink.* 17 Nov 2014. Web.

Roti Prata

Balamurugan, Anasuya. "Roti prata" National Library Board, *Singapore Infopedia.* 2010. Web.

Başan, Ghillie and Tan, Terry. *Classic Recipes, Tastes & Traditions of Malaysia & Singapore.* London: Lorenz, 2008. Print.

Chan, Margaret. *Margaret Chan's Foodstops.* Singapore: Landmark Books, 1992. Print.

Panickar, Gayathri. "Prata paradise." Tabla, 19 Jul 2013: 1, 14-15. *Newslink.* 17 Nov 2014. Web.

Phoon, Audrey. "Flipping Out Over Prata." *The Business Times,* 20 Feb 2010. *Newslink.* 17 Nov 2014. Web.

Pomeroy, Ben. "Roti, Shark, and Buss-Up Shot: Get to know the Trinidadian Food of NYC." *Serious Eats.* 19 Mar 2014. <http://newyork.seriouseats.com/2014/03/best-trinidadian-caribbean-food-nyc.html> 17 Nov 2014. Web.

Pyler, Ernst John. *Baking Science and Technology.* Kansas: Sosland, 1988. Print.

Sanmugam, Devagi. *Indian Heritage Cooking.* Singapore: Marshall Cavendish Cuisine, 2011. Print.

Tee, Hun Ching. "Prata Ra-Ra." *The Straits Times,* 29 Apr 2001: 10. *Newslink.* 17 Nov 2014. Web.

"Try the savory ..." *The Straits Times,* 26 Jul 2009: 19. *Newslink.* 17 Nov 2014. Web.

Desserts

Bubor Cha Cha

Leong, Yee Soo. *The Best of Singapore's Recipes: Everyday Favourites.* Singapore: Times Edition, 2004. Print.

Tan, Sylvia. *Singapore Heritage Food.* Singapore: Landmark Books, 2004. Print.

Tan, Cecilia. *Penang Nyonya Cooking.* Singapore: Times Books International, 1983. Print.

Xu, Jianteng, Xiaoyu Su, Soyoung Lim, Jason Griffin, Edward Carey, Benjamin Katz, John Tomich, Scott Smith, and Weiqun Wang. "Characterisation and Stability of Anthocyanins in Purple-Fleshed Sweet Potato P40." *Food Chemistry* (2014). Print.

Chendol

"A Malaysian notebook" *The Straits Times,* 19 Dec 1953: 8. 19 Nov 2014. Web.

Brown, Amy. *Understanding Food: Principles and Preparation.* California: Wadsworth Thomson Learning, 2000. Print.

Jane, Jay-lin. "Structural features of starch granules II." *Starch: Chemistry and Technology, 3rd Edition (pp 193-236).* Ed. James N. BeMiller and Roy L. Whistler. Massachusetts: Academic Press, 2009. 193-236. Print.

McWilliams, Margaret. *Foods: Experimental Perspectives,* 7th edition. New Jersey: Pearson Education, 2012. Print.

"Soon the sick won't have to travel in pig baskets." *The Straits Times,* 8 May 1952: 8. 19 Nov 2014. Web.

Tan, Florence. *Secrets of Nyonya Cooking.* Singapore: Times Editions, 2001. Print.

Ondeh Ondeh

"A Taste of Indonesia." *The Daily Examiner* 1 Oct 2013: 18. *LexisNexis Academic.* 17 Nov 2014. Web.

"Lifestyle's Top 8 Ondeh Ondeh." *The Straits Times,* 27 Aug 2006: L24. *Newslink.* 17 Nov 2014. Web.

Teo, Pau Lin. "The best onde onde in town." *The Straits Times,* 27 Aug 2006: L24. *NewspaperSG.* 17 Nov 2014. Web.

Tan, Rebecca Lynne. "Deli Maslina." *The Straits Times,* 5 Sep 2010: 22. *Newslink.* 17 Nov 2014. Web.

Tan, Teck Heng. "Edgy Remixes on a Plate." *The Business Times,* 6 Aug 2011: L8-L9. *Newslink.* 17 Nov 2014. Web.

Tau Suan with Dough Fritters

McWilliams, Margaret. *Foods: Experimental Perspectives.* 7th ed. New Jersey: Pearson Prentice Hall, 2012. Print.

Tan, Terry, et al. *Shiok!: Exciting Tropical Asian Flavors.* Singapore: Periplus Editions, 2003. Print.

THE TEAM

Catch a glimpse behind the scenes
of the Diploma in Baking and Culinary Science team:

Front row (from left): Alvin Tan, Gary Lim, Petrina Lim, Randy Chow, Roger Low, Paul Sin
Back row (from left): Candy Tay, Emma Choondee, Zhang Yu, Natalie Oh, Jolene Lim

Project Lead	Petrina Lim
Food Science and Nutrition	Paul Sin, Zhang Yu, Emma Choondee and Candy Tay
Food Preparation and Styling	Randy Chow, Gary Lim and Roger Low
Singapore Heritage and Food Culture	Alvin Tan, Chia Wei Fun, Serene Cai, Tan Han Yong and Loh Hui Hong
Sketch Illustrations	Kenneth Chin
Marketing and Publicity	Petrina Lim, Zhang Yu and Emma Choondee